The Green Mister Rogers

Children's Literature
Association Series

The Green Mister Rogers

Environmentalism in Mister Rogers' Neighborhood

Sara Lindey and **Jason King**
Foreword by Junlei Li

University Press of Mississippi / Jackson

The University Press of Mississippi is the scholarly publishing agency of the Mississippi Institutions of Higher Learning: Alcorn State University, Delta State University, Jackson State University, Mississippi State University, Mississippi University for Women, Mississippi Valley State University, University of Mississippi, and University of Southern Mississippi.

www.upress.state.ms.us

The University Press of Mississippi is a member of the Association of University Presses.

All images and lyrics appear courtesy of the Fred Rogers Company.

Copyright © 2022 by University Press of Mississippi
All rights reserved

First printing 2022
∞

Library of Congress Control Number: 2021042891
Hardback ISBN 978-1-4968-3662-5
Epub single ISBN 978-1-4968-3663-2
Epub institutional ISBN 978-1-4968-3665-6
PDF single ISBN 978-1-4968-3666-3
PDF institutional ISBN 1-4968-3667-0

British Library Cataloging-in-Publication Data available

For our children:
Pete & Andy, and Colleen, Thomas, & Benjamin

"What does make the difference between wishing and realizing our wishes? Lots of things, of course, but the main one, I think, is whether we link our wishes to our hopes and our hopes to our active striving. It might take months or years for a wish to come true, but it's far more likely to happen when you care so much about it that you'll do all you can to make it happen."

—**Fred Rogers**, University of Indianapolis commencement address, 1988

Contents

xi   Foreword

3   Introduction: Fred Rogers's Ecological Imagination

21   Chapter 1. Make-Believe and Reality: Rogers's Apocalyptic Environmentalism

43   Chapter 2. The Art of Environmentalism: Integral Ecology in Fred Rogers's Neighborhoods

63   Chapter 3. Puppets and Animal Wisdom: Ecological Conversion

83   Chapter 4. Playthings and Creativity: Reduce, Reuse, Recycle, and Co-Create

105   Chapter 5. "Tree Tree Tree": The Joy in Rogers's Ecological Worldview

125   Conclusion: Fred Rogers and Environmental Wisdom

113   Appendix

145 Acknowledgments

149 Notes

159 Bibliography

169 Index

Foreword

There is a very special room on the second floor of the Fred Rogers Center, located on the campus of Saint Vincent College, in the small town of Latrobe, Pennsylvania. Its southward windows stretch from floor to ceiling and overlook a nature reserve, protected and kept wild and beautiful by another honorable and respected Latrobe family—Arnie (who played golf with Fred as a child and went on to greater achievements in that field) and Winnie Palmer. When the sunlight beams through the windows, it illuminates a restored Steinway piano on which Fred Rogers played, composed, and mused since he was a ten-year-old boy. Above the piano, an oil painting of Fred shows him smiling, as if into the television camera to millions of children, as he ties his iconic tennis shoes.

In addition to the ambience, what makes this room special is that it is quite literally designed as "Fred's room." In the early 2000s, after Fred Rogers retired from television, he wondered what he might do for this new phase of his life and work. Persuaded by his trusted friends and colleagues, including Milton Chen (the executive director of the George Lucas Foundation) and Archabbot Douglas of Saint Vincent Archabbey (a clinical psychologist who was Fred's close friend for more than two decades), Fred had consented to continuing his work through the Fred Rogers Center. He would finally be able to take the time to organize and synthesize his life's work, teach new generations of college students across disciplines about human development, and continue spreading the messages of the Neighborhood beyond the television screen. As the architects of the building drew up the plans, they built a room where Fred would reflect, write, and stay during the week (his apartment was more than an hour away in Pittsburgh). That room eventually became the "Gathering Space." This is where teachers, students, guests, and neighbors gather when they visit the Fred Rogers Center. This is where they talk about Fred Rogers—the past, present, and future of his legacy.

I remember one of these conversations vividly. I was still fairly new as the co-director at the Fred Rogers Center. Across the table was Sara Lindey, an English professor with a specialization in children's literature and the lead author of this book you hold. In the years past, I looked up to Fred as someone who took the science of child development and put it into practice and public service. Diving into the Fred Rogers Archive (located in a temperature controlled room just below us, housing over 20,000 items from Fred's life and work), I began to understand that while Fred chose to serve young children, the ideas he brought to the television screen were rooted in a much deeper and ageless foundation. Similarly, Sara had spent a good deal of time studying Fred's work and developed a curriculum around how to extend and reapply Fred's ideas to present day education. I listened with great interest to all the things that Sara saw in Fred's work and the many ways she used the archives. Fred was speaking about and for all human beings. In Sara, I found a kindred spirit whose academic interest was rooted in children and who also discovered the larger scope of Fred's vision. At the culminating point of the conversation, Sara proclaimed with her characteristic enthusiasm, "Fred is a public intellectual! He should be studied, not just by educators, but by everyone! He's like Emerson. He's like Martin Luther King. We ought to have a Society for the Study of Fred Rogers!" Her excitement and seriousness were contagious. I never forgot the scholarly vision she was beginning to sketch out. Fred's work is to be studied. Fred's message is to be extended. Fred's legacy belongs to the public, not just an archive.

In the years since then, I witnessed the public embrace of Fred Rogers through the particularly tumultuous political and social upheavals for the late 2010s. A documentary about Fred's work became the highest-grossing biographical documentary of all time. A Hollywood version of Fred's friendship with a journalist reached theaters worldwide. In between, an authorized biography of Fred Rogers was published. Through it all, I was reminded of my conversation with Sara. Fred is a public intellectual! He belongs to everyone!

In this book, Sara and her colleague Jason King, a professor of theology at Saint Vincent College, took just one single five-episode theme week and demonstrated that it is possible to learn, to discover, to understand, and to connect Fred's ideas to how we learn and live as human beings today. They used their scholarly lens—literary, theological, social, and political—to weave together the visible parts of Fred's work on television to the less visible but essential parts of Fred's thinking in his speeches and notes. They showed what it means to take Fred's work—and words—seriously. By doing so, they opened the door to an endless possibility. If it is possible to learn this much from just five episodes, what more can we discover in the 895 episodes of *Mister Rogers' Neighborhood* and the 20,000 artifacts carefully stored and catalogued in the Fred Rogers Archive?

I will not spoil for the reader what is in the book. What I can say is that when I read through the early draft, I had to slow myself down. On every other page, something would catch my eye and made me stop and think. It may be a familiar Fred Rogers quote explained in a new way, or a new quote connected to all the familiar ideas, or a meaningful detail from an episode that I have overlooked or would not have ever noticed. I found myself highlighting and underlining the passages, even took pictures of some pages on my phone so I could have it handy to read whenever I thought about Fred's work.

Of all the theme weeks, I am grateful that Sara and Jason choose the 1990 week on "Caring for the Environment." Even as the publisher readies this book for publication, wildfires rage along the West Coast and coat the sky an ominous orange from Los Angles to Portland, while hurricanes stampede against the Gulf Coast. The tireless zoologist and advocate Jane Goodall observed sharply, "Human beings are the only species that will destroy the only home it has." There is a better way. There has to be a better way. Fred was trying to tell us that thirty years ago. We can still hear the message today if we open our hearts and ears, thanks to the meticulous research and the imaginative connections included in this book.

Some readers may find it a little jarring that I have been using the first name "Fred" in this foreword instead of "Mister Rogers." When I worked and taught at the Fred Rogers Center, my colleagues and I discussed this carefully and decided that we will refer to "Mister Rogers" whenever we are talking about the television program, and "Fred" whenever we are referring to the thoughtful human being whose thinking, imagining, and praying inspired the program. In the same way, this book by Sara and Jason is about "Fred." It pulled open the small sliding curtains that separated the puppets in the Neighborhood of Make-Believe and the famous puppeteer behind the set and gave all of us a glimpse of the coherent vision behind the beloved children's program.

More than being revered or remembered, I believe Fred Rogers wanted to be taken seriously. While he chose to serve young children and families with his life's work, he set his eyes upon the larger human neighborhood. In some interviews, I heard Fred say, with almost imperceptible impatience and ever-so-slight irritation, that his program was not just for "little children." It is also for all who have since grown up with the neighborhood, who have children of their own, who have power—and responsibility—over the world. I read this book as an encouragement for all of us who have deep affections for Fred Rogers's work to take its messages seriously. If we read it carefully, we will find that *Mister Rogers' Neighborhood* was about every single one of us, at whatever age, building and nurturing relationships with our neighbors, our environment, and ourselves.

In a public service announcement after September 11, 2001, Fred Rogers spoke gently and seriously to all the grown-ups about the

Hebrew phrase "Tikkun olam," reminding us that we are *all* called to be "repairers of creation." Fred died in 2003 and was not able to use the Gathering Space to continue speaking to us. So, here we are, gathered through a book, learning to mend our neighborhoods.

JUNLEI LI

The Green
Mister Rogers

Introduction

Fred Rogers's Ecological Imagination

We'd like to ask you to think about Fred Rogers as one of the key figures in our history. Like Ralph Waldo Emerson and Martin Luther King Jr., he was an American minister who has had a profound influence on the shape of our culture. The seeds he has planted take root and his words, like Walt Whitman's poetry, have the power to bring us "good health" and "filter and fibre our blood." Gavin Edwards, in *Kindness and Wonder: Why Mister Rogers Matters Now More Than Ever*, asserts that we remember what Rogers taught us, even if we don't remember that the lessons came from him. We hope you review some episodes of Rogers's television program, but agree with Edwards when he states, "you don't need to binge-watch the series to renew yourself, because if you ever spent time with the show, you carry the Neighborhood wherever you go." We hope that Rogers's words, his speeches, sermons, and television program will remain visible in future generations. While this moment, with the film, documentary, biographies, podcasts, journalism, and memes abounding, we hope to join a chorus that sings of Fred Rogers's depths and relevance to move past a nostalgia that reduces Rogers to an interesting historical figure. Instead, as Edwards puts it, we are after a "'nostalgia' [that] is just another way to spell 'cultural legacy.' [because] At the moment you are reading this book, Mister Rogers has enough purchase on your heart to change the society you live in."

Rogers offers a vision to fortify us to work together. Rogers reveals the truth about our world, about ourselves. As he shows this world to us, he helps us build it collaboratively. Rogers celebrates the accident of place, which brings people together in neighborhoods of care, ecosystems of cohabitation. His insistence on the dignity of each and every valuable person proposes a radical empathy and a revolutionary ethics. His imagination penetrates the smallest details, looks inside our emotional and imaginative lives, affirms each individual self, and continually expands compassion to every corner of creation. Rogers's contagious perspective propels trust and inspires joy. For now, you are reading a book about how Rogers's expressed his ideas about environmentalism.

The Invisible Essentials:
Fred Rogers as Educator, Pastor, Artist

Fred Rogers was an international celebrity. He was a pioneer in children's television, an advocate for families, and a multimedia artist and performer. He wrote the television scripts and music, performed puppetry, sang, and hosted *Mister Rogers' Neighborhood*. The show reached generations of viewers from its nationally syndicated run from 1968 to 2001. It won a Peabody Award and four Emmy Awards and received twenty-five Emmy Award nominations. In 1997, Fred Rogers received Emmy's lifetime achievement award. He wrote, directed, and starred in almost 900 episodes over the span of more than thirty years! In fact, in the 1980s, at its height, *Mister Rogers Neighborhood* reached nearly 10 percent of American households! His television program continues to touch many families with its continued availability on media streaming services.

Rogers earned a bachelor's in music composition from Rollins College, Florida, was ordained as a Presbyterian minister from

Pittsburgh Theological Seminary, and studied with Dr. Margaret McFarland at the University of Pittsburgh's Graduate School of Child Development. Rogers brought all his talents, studies, and ambition to his work to serve children. Biographer Maxwell King articulates two compelling reasons why Fred Rogers and his work deserve critical attention today. To quote at length:

> First, [Rogers] recognized the critical importance of learning during the earliest years. No one better understood how essential it is for proper social, emotional, cognitive, and language development to take place in the first few years of life. And no one did more to convince a mass audience in America of the value of early education.
>
> Second, he provided, and continues to provide, exemplary moral leadership. Fred Rogers advanced humanistic values because of his belief in Christianity, but his spirituality was completely eclectic; he found merit in all faiths and philosophies. His signature value was human kindness; he lived it and he preached it, to children, to their parents, to their teachers, to all of us everywhere who could take the time to listen.

We'd like to add a third reason: Rogers is a multimedia artist whose creative endeavors and imaginative spirit infuse his work with emotional sophistication and deep social and political relevance. He is an innovator in children's media. The quality of his narratives, the fullness of his motifs, the coordination among side-plots to spin out different ways to contemplate his theme, the music, puppets, and personal performance in *Mister Rogers' Neighborhood* are stunning. While Rogers's work might seem quiet and understated, look again. His imaginative work is clever and intricate, infused with contagious curiosity and joy. Fred Rogers is a public intellectual, a spiritual leader, and a creative artist.

Rogers insisted that children deserve the best possible television programing, repeatedly and stubbornly insisting on perfection from everyone who worked with him. During an "Invisible to the Eye" talk he gave at the Johnson & Johnson executive luncheon in 1994, Rogers told one such story about producing children's programming in Madras, India. Rogers explains that he demands quality television and asks, "What will it take for our *whole* society to insist on the best for children?" Rogers often told the story of a gifted sculptor who, as the father of one of the kindergarteners Rogers visited during his practicum work in child development, would come to class weekly to show his artistry. Rogers explained, "He didn't *teach* about clay, he just loved it and fashioned it and showed how he could express his feelings with it in that place where children could watch him. And little by little the children themselves began to love *their* clay and what it felt like to work with it and what they found they could make of it." Rogers insists that the best way to teach children is to love what you do and give children a gift of that love; this is a directive Rogers lived by in his own television work. His example might be true, but it's also symbolic; the power to create from clay sounds biblical, doesn't it?

After relaying a touching story about his Aunt Alberta Rogers's funeral in which her four-year-old granddaughter performed cartwheels as a way to deal with her loss and celebrate Aunt Bert's life, Rogers concludes: "My hunch is that if we allow ourselves to give who *we* really are to the children in our lives, give them the invisible essentials of who we are, we will in some way inspire cartwheels in their hearts." Rogers's lectures, like his children's program, are small masterpieces; this one, like many others explicates his "invisible essentials" theme. And Rogers lives out his own imperatives. Rogers gave his authentic self in love and in joy to generations of children.

In addressing children, Rogers's mainstay is emotional and spiritual fortification that enables campaigns for social justice. Michael Long, author of *Peaceful Neighbor: Discovering the Countercultural Mister Rogers*, argues that Rogers tirelessly produced children's media and television specials that worked toward a pacifist intervention for social justice. Long calls Rogers a "radical Christian pacifist" and "fierce peacemaker" as he places Rogers in his political and religious context to show how "Rogers's spiritual beliefs led him to oppose all wars as well as all barriers to individual and social peace." Discussing Rogers in the context of the Vietnam War, Gulf War, civil rights era, and other historical and political flash points, Long maintains that Rogers's ordination as a Presbyterian minister, combined with his religious conviction, fueled his messaging for children and families. He asserts that Rogers "fervently believed in a God who accepts us as we are and loves us without condition, who is present in each person and all of creation, and who desires a world marked by peace and wholeness. With this progressive spirituality as his inspiration, Rogers fashioned his children's program as a platform for sharing countercultural beliefs about caring nonviolently for one another, animals, and the earth."

Rogers's own spiritual refrain comes from a secular source: *The Little Prince*, a novella that reads as a fable. Antoine de Saint-Exupéry, a French author, airplane pilot, and war hero, published his children's story in 1943, appearing both in the original French and English translation. It is the story of a child from his own personal planet who journeys to other worlds to escape from his troubles with his own planet and its tender rose, and to explore and learn and search for a friend. Instead, the Little Prince discovers that the grown-ups he encounters have little to teach him: they are governed by greed and envy; they are myopic and selfish. On Earth, a fox wants to love the Little Prince and so teaches the Little Prince how to tame him. In this trusting relationship, the Little Prince discovers how each individual is special, valuable, and lovable. This is a lesson about love, and it is both a great comfort as well as a source for sorrow when the Little Prince and narrator are confronted with the inevitability of loss and death.

Rogers's favorite quotation from *The Little Prince*, which he often cited and kept framed in his office, reads: "*L'essentiel est invisible pour les yeux*." In English, the full passage reads, from the mouth of the fox: "Here is my secret. It's quite simple: one sees clearly only with the heart. Anything essential is invisible to the eye." Rogers repeats the Little Prince's message to the narrator with his own translation—"That which is essential is invisible to the eye"—making it the subject or germ of many of his lectures. Rogers uses Saint-Exupéry's maxim to spin out multiple, intersecting understandings of its spiritual and practical truth.

For example, Rogers began speeches to early childhood educators and corporate executives (the "Invisible to the Eye" lecture cited above) with the exact same introduction about *The Little Prince*:

> On the walls of our Family Communications offices are reminders of who we are and what we do: photographs, drawings and paintings from children, along with letters from parents about ordinary and extraordinary needs. There's the Boise Peace Quilt and a wooden plaque with the Greek word for "grace" carved in it. And, there's a framed pieced of calligraphy with the quotation from *The Little Prince*, "That which is essential is invisible to the eye."

Rogers dilates on the quotation, explaining that professionals who educate and care for children have "a special calling" that has a lot to do with "what's invisible to the eye:" namely, "the heads and hearts of the next generation: the thoughts and feelings of the future." Here, Rogers explicitly names what is invisible: one's head and heart, one's imagination and feelings. And these two parts of people's interiority are deeply and inextricably connected.

Of course, anyone familiar with Rogers understands that helping children with their emotional development, understanding the invisible activity of the head and heart, is his primary value. One has only to think of the famous 1969 Senate hearing where Rogers's short, six-minute appeal to Senator John Pastore helped earned the Public Broadcasting Service $20 million in funding. Rogers explains what *Mister Rogers' Neighborhood* accomplishes:

> I give an expression of care every day to each child, to help him realize that he is unique. I end the program by saying, "You've made

this day a special day, by just your being you. There's no person in the whole world like you, and I like you, just the way you are." And I feel that if we in public television can only make it clear that feelings are mentionable and manageable, we will have done a great service for mental health. I think that it's much more dramatic that two men could be working out their feelings of anger—much more dramatic than showing something of gunfire. I'm constantly concerned about what our children are seeing, and for fifteen years I have tried in this country and Canada, to present what I feel is a meaningful expression of care.

Rogers then says the lyrics of "What Do You Do with the Mad That You Feel?," which tells children that they can always stop whatever they think they might regret doing and do something more constructive with their anger. But it's not just anger, of course, but any number of feelings.

The greatest and most powerful invisible feeling, for Rogers, might be love. It is this feeling which he reflects on at length in many speeches and within *Mister Rogers' Neighborhood*. When addressing "the heads and hearts of the next generation" in his commencement address for Thiel College in 1969, "Encouraging Creativity," Rogers underscores the invisible essential of love. He defines "the true meaning of love" and examines its power:

Love is generally confused with dependence. Those of us who have grown in true love know that we can love only in proportion to our capacity for independence. We must be able to be ourselves in the face of love for our love to have meaning. Only by understanding our own uniqueness can we fully appreciate how special our neighbor really is. Only by being aware of our own endowments can we begin to marvel at the variety which our Creator has provided in men. And as we do marvel we will find ourselves being concerned about the conditions that make life on earth possible, we will recognize the need to make people more important than things, and we will join hands with young and old alike by putting our dominant energies into developing a sane design for living.

For Rogers, a person's invisible inner strength is based in self-love which allows them to follow their inner voices, understand their own selves, and "grow in wisdom [. . . and] in the joy and the dignity of being truly human." For Rogers, the force of human love is understood in its relation to God's love.

In a 1997 address to the Memphis Theological Seminary called "Invisible Essentials," Rogers offers a treatise that seems to prove that God's love is part and parcel of human love. As he congratulates the efforts of the Memphis Theological Seminary, he reveals what he finds is best in religious education is the same sort of secular gospel he's been preaching on *Mister Rogers' Neighborhood*. After singing "It's You I Like," he characterizes God's invisible "mind and heart" in the same way he characterizes human being's invisible essentials in his lectures to childhood educators and corporate executives: "For many years this school has been helping people to become advocates for the most essential good news in all of history: the news that in the mind and heart of the eternal, we human beings have value, that we are partners with God in forgiveness and that the space between any two of us is holy ground." Rogers merges his way of talking about human beings and love, his own vocabulary and phrases, with a way to understand God's love and how it invisibly acts between people in the real, tangible world. He concludes:

> May this theological seminary here in Memphis continue to announce to the world that it's never too late to embrace the one who loves what is absolutely essential about us—that that advocate, Jesus the Christ, accepts us exactly as we are—invisible to the eye—and invites us to grow right along with him forever.
>
> Let us pray: Immortal, invisible God, help us to want to do your will and to *do* it well in all the neighborhoods of your world: through Jesus the Christ our lord, amen.

Rogers's prayer aligns the invisibility of human interiority with God's immortal invisibility. He affirms the seminarian graduates' ability to create, with God, a world in harmony with God's love.

In this monumental lecture, which is both a kind of sermon and a commencement address, delivered to graduating seminarians, Rogers identifies three discrete "invisible essentials": one, the human person; two, the space between people, which he repeatedly over the years characterizes as "holy ground"; and, three, in his simple but deep way, God.

William Guy, in "The Theology of *Mister Rogers' Neighborhood*," asserts that Rogers's "love-ethic" relies on "a system of circulation" among the self, the other, and God. He maintains that Rogers's affirmations of love have two components: "one of *grace* (the gift, the confirmation of one's own unique importance) and one of *claim* (the need to become aware of other people's needs, which are like one's own)." These two parts work together in "an ethic of challenge and responsibility." And, what enables that work, that circulating love, is the invisible holy ground between people. This invisible holy ground reveals a spiritual truth that exposes the complexity of Rogers's theology: individuals are not alone nor autonomous but exist in cooperative and interdependent relationships. As Guy puts it, for Rogers, "Paradoxically one *can* have it all, it would seem, but only after one has recognized one's own limits, surrendered any claim to total self-sufficiency." For Rogers, the individual is rare, valuable, lovable, loving, connected, and interdependent.

Rogers makes it clear that the invisible space between people is of preeminent importance in his commencement address at Saint Vincent College in 2000. While he doesn't use the exact words "holy ground" to describe the space between people, he clearly describes the invisible space between grateful individuals as a place where an invisible God is made present. Rogers explains that it might not matter if we recognize that God is acting between us because, regardless, he believes it is a fact of our existence. Rogers explains that his impulse to bow in gratitude is an impulse to acknowledge the divine:

What I've come to understand is that we who bow are probably—whether we know it or not—acknowledging the presence of the sacred: we're bowing to the sacred in our neighbor. You see, I believe that appreciation is a holy thing, that when we look for what's best in the person we happen to be with at the moment, we're doing what God does all the time. So, in loving and appreciating our neighbor, we're participating in something extremely sacred."

After mentioning Saint-Exupéry's message ("What is essential is invisible to the eye"), Rogers asserts, "I feel the closer we get to knowing and living the truth of that sentence, the closer we get to wisdom." It's touching to see and hear Rogers talk in person with the young adults that he probably visited with when they were children watching *Mister Rogers' Neighborhood*. Rogers cultivates the invisible holy ground between his childhood television neighbor and the now-grown graduates by making space and time for it.

Rogers shifts from the invisible appreciation and gratefulness that has been the study of his speech to the people who live out those values and feelings, saying to the graduates, "I'd like to give you all an invisible gift; a gift of silence to think about those who nourish you at the deepest part of your being ... anyone who has ever loved you and wanted what was best for you in life." Rogers opens up and multiplies the idea of invisible essentials to include silence and the people who are far away, or in "Heaven." Rogers closes his talk by referring back to *The Little Prince*:

> So in the midst of this community of Saint Vincent which has always majored in hospitality, my prayer for you is that you will take good care of that part of you—that invisible part of you where your best dreams come from, that part of you that helps you to feel for others ... and allows you to appreciate your life and encourages you to bow to your neighbor in that sacred space between grateful hearts.
>
> That's what will matter most in our world.
> We're certainly counting on you.
> Congratulations!"

Rogers reiterates the idea of the sacred ground between people and his trusts that this particular group of young adults have the wisdom to do well in their own lives and in making the world a better place. Rogers has faith.

All in all, Rogers proposes that if we can understand the invisible thoughts and feelings of ourselves then we can live and act in the strength of our self-love, turn in love toward others who are our neighbors, and circulate God's love among people, creatures, and the natural world. In short, Rogers's invisible essentials transform our selves, our lives, and our worlds. Guy asserts that Rogers's theological perspective is not naïve. In discussing *Mister Rogers' Neighborhood*, Guy states, "one can positively have one's breath taken away by the metaphysical openness and daring of some of the show's episodes, by the willingness to face abysses that various shows embody." He sums up Rogers's triumphant spiritual force that trusts the strength of an invisible God and the influence and energy of human beings' invisible love. Guy explains:

> The point here is simply that the freedom to see life as providing good feelings, which Mister Rogers enacts and invites his viewers to share in, the zest for living that he advocates, is not bought cheaply or dishonestly, at the expense of sweeping certain harsh truths or certain obstacles under the rug. The vision of Mister Rogers has been honestly earned. It has been built up over the weeks, months, and years by giving a fair reflection of life, both its good and its bad. [. . .] He has not shuffled the data in order to come by his results.

Guy powerfully illustrates Rogers's theology while honoring the secular way he talks about it.

Mister Rogers' Neighborhood is also a place where invisible essentials are lived out, dramatized, and rehearsed. In some of his later lectures he includes video clips of *Mister Rogers' Neighborhood*. For example, in the "Invisible to the Eye" speech he gave to a group of corporate executives that begins this section, Rogers shows some *Neighborhood* segments featuring musicians Yo-Yo Ma and Ella

Jenkins expressing and giving their inner selves in their artistry. Rogers uses these videos to help show the meaning and value of invisible essentials. His children's program is easily employed in his lectures to adults.

Chris Buczinsky argues that the children's program "*Mister Rogers Neighborhood* is best seen as a witness to the enduring appeal of the Christian pastoral [. . .] One might call his program twentieth-century America's most successful religious mission." However, instead of speaking bluntly or assertively about his faith, Roger weaves his spiritual, religious, and theological understandings into everything he says no matter if he's talking to seminarians, media executives, celebrities, politicians, educators, college students, or young children. His sermons, commencement addresses, conference speeches, and talk on children's television is harmonious in its messaging, its delivery and style, and, most importantly, its content. He never tries to use his faith as a means to divide but rather to unite. In *Mister Rogers' Neighborhood's* "Caring for the Environment" series, Rogers's brings all his spiritual, intellectual, and creative values together.

"Caring for the Environment": Celebrations of Connectivity and Interdependence

Originally airing the week before the Sunday, April 22, Earth Day, the five-episode series from 1990 entitled "Caring for the Environment" (#1616–1620) coalesces with a global initiative celebrating the twentieth anniversary of the first Earth Day. In a pamphlet for parents and educators that supports the episode in which Mister Rogers visits a recycling center, Rogers, in his opening letter, explains his perspective:

> Concepts such as scarcity, recycling, and conservation are hard ones for children, who understand best what they can see and touch. It may even be hard to convince them of the earth's limited resources

when, to them, it may seem that there is so much of everything all around! I don't believe it's helpful to make young children *worry* about environmental problems, or to make them feel *they* are responsible for solving those problems. It's enough, I believe, to help children understand more about their world and to encourage them, very early in their lives, to care for the people and things in it.

Rogers continues by encouraging teachers and parents to show by example their love and wonder at nature and their ecological practices, such as turning off lights and recycling. While these activities might sound simple, Rogers asserts that a focus on cultivating an ecological consciousness grounded and fortified in care and love can return to us a better world. He closes his letter thus:

Of course it's your continual care for the children themselves that helps them develop a sense that they are loved, lovable, and capable of loving. From that, they can go on to grow into adults who rejoice in life and regard this planet with loving care. They'll be the ones who will find it natural in their own tomorrows to recycle and reuse materials, marvel at flowers, and turn off the lights.

Rogers hopes that families who talk about the "Caring for the Environment" programs make the world a better place.

The dramas in "Caring for the Environment" are rich with conflict and urgency as well as hope and care. In these episodes, Rogers uses the Neighborhood of Make-Believe segments to dramatize an environmental disaster: the regional dumps are overflowing and trash swiftly accumulates around the neighborhood. Rogers shows neighbors struggling with the crisis and eventually reaching a solution when their Northwood neighbor goats agree to help them separate the trash so it can be processed by another neighbor's newly invented recycling machine. Rogers reflects on pretend play in discussion and song in his comfortable living room. He also includes field trips to a recycling center as well as visits to an artist's studio where every day refuse is transformed into bricolage artwork, a visit with a real goat, and a visit with oceanographer Sylvia Earle to Florida's Laguna Key coral reefs to learn about the ocean habitat, which is implicated as a possible new site for trash in the Neighborhood of Make-Believe's overwhelming trash cataclysm. Ensconced in the safety of Rogers's domestic space, Rogers introduces children to a wider world, expanding their sense of care.

We might say, using Kamala Platt's term, that Rogers's "Caring for the Environment" week qualifies as "environmental justice poetics," which she describes as texts "created to promote both environmental wellbeing and social justice." While *Mister Rogers' Neighborhood*'s "Caring for the Environment" programs might not meet Platt's criterion as texts that "expose environmental racism and the closely linked degradation of the earth," Rogers does offer up a plot within the week about the threats to fish in Florida's coral reef and animals in Someplace Else. Thus, Rogers points children towards a sophisticated critique of the speciesism and classism that Platt prioritizes.

Regarding environmental consciousness in particular, Rogers focuses on children's imaginative and spiritual understandings while including some attention to behavior to help children live out their ideas, values, and convictions. As Sidney Dobrin and Kenneth Kidd explain in *Wild Things: Children's Culture and Ecocriticism*, scholars, educators, and children's literature writers and media producers agree "both that children are naturally closer to nature and that nature education, even intervention, is in order" operating with "the consensus belief across narrative genres that even if the child has a privileged relationship with nature, he or she must be educated into a deeper—or at least different—awareness." "Caring for the Environment" operates in accord with those twinned insights. Rogers intentionally, consciously, and thoroughly advocates for a deeper understanding of our place in the world. His television program speaks to children about their own bodies, hearts, and minds in relation to their home neighborhood, their regional green spaces, and their Earth.

In this book, we catalogue and expand upon the various ways Rogers dramatizes connections, particularly exploring the dimensions of his ecological imagination. In chapter one, we examine the apocalyptic narrative in this week's Neighborhood of Make-Believe. Here, a trash calamity swiftly unfolds. It shuts down Harriet Elizabeth Cow's school and Donkey Hodie's farm and prompts Cornelius S. Pecially's factory to stop production on rocking chairs to make nose muffs that help protect neighbors from the oppressive garbage smells. The catastrophe expands to the cities of Southwood and Westwood. Many neighbors pitch in to help, from the intergalactic television show *The Universe Today* to puppet Hilda Dingleboarder's recycling machine to the neighboring goats' recycling plan. Rogers's revelatory vision helps us to see ourselves connected to others so that we might care for others as we care for ourselves.

Throughout the week of "Caring for the Environment," showing children the connections to others is one of the most prominent themes. In chapter two, we focus on how Rogers uses artwork to imagine and remember the connections between people, animals, and their homes. Through his fish postcard, photographs of fish, and artist Leo Sewell's fish sculpture, Rogers uses art to link children to fish and children's home with the coral reef. He allows space for anxieties around pollution while exposing a world populated with grown-up heroes and helpers he meets during a visit to Florida's coral reef. Using fish artwork to pivot between what we can see and what we can imagine and remember, Rogers expands children's care for their home to care for fish and their homes—and, implicitly, all animals and their habitats—and so forges a bond between them.

Rogers's puppets expand these connections of care even further. In chapter three, we focus on how Rogers's puppets deepen emotional and empathetic capabilities to empower children. The Neighborhood of Make-Believe is filled with interspecies kin, with animals, puppets, humans, and humans dressed as animals all living together, and many part of the same family. Through puppets, parts of human beings are externalized and embodied in other creatures. Rogers suggests that children come to see aspects of themselves in everyone and everything around them. In this way, Ropers suggests that puppets expand children's feelings and so expand their circle of concern. More and more creatures and things are connected to the child.

Even the toys Rogers uses during this week of programs connect children to the world around them. In chapter four, we catalogue the homemade toys in "Caring for the Environment" to analyze how play can realize and thematize recycling. For example, Rogers takes a ball and bag and turns them into a game. It is fun, but it is also about seeing things in new ways. Discarded household objects are no longer trash but pieces of a child's joyful world. It is the same with Rogers's toy blocks. He has a wooden puzzle that evokes reflections on the complex interactions within us and outside of us. The toy is a conduit that links the inner life of the child to the puzzle to the trees and to the people who made the toy. Rogers even shows how children could use cardboard boxes and homemade puppets to put on a television show like his own, extending and capitalizing on children's connection even to Mister Rogers.

In chapter five, we take a broader view, locating in the song "Tree Tree Tree" Rogers's longstanding interest in connections between people, places, animals, plants, and things. The song is used to show that children and parents are still connected, even when parents have to leave to go to work. It is played by Yo-Yo Ma on the cello and by Handyman Negri and friends using pipes, screwdrivers, and a handsaw. It is sung by Rogers and Queen Sara but also by Barbara Koski in Finnish and Peter Ostroushko in Ukrainian. This song about the natural world forges bonds between family members and cultures. Through this song, along with puppets, art, and toys, Rogers shows an interconnected world, one of ever-expanding care.

Rogers's environmental imagination is an expression of his "invisible essentials." Rogers presents a world where children learn why and how to care for creation and so have the foundation to become adults who act for the good of the environment. Yet, Rogers insists on protecting children and preparing them. In greater measure, Rogers's program attends to the caretakers watching and learning alongside the children. Rogers reminds parents of their capabilities and responsibilities, assuring us that we, too, are lovable and capable of loving, and all but demanding that we get busy on the work we have to do.

Chapter One

Make-Believe and Reality
Rogers's Apocalyptic Environmentalism

In *Mister Rogers' Neighborhood*, trips to the Neighborhood of Make-Believe can get pretty wild. In the weeklong "Caring for the Environment" series, trash crowds the Neighborhood of Make-Believe with dirty garbage cans smelling so badly everyone wears nose muffs and Handyman Negri spends his time fanning the stench to the sky. Neighbor Aber appears in a wetsuit complete with fins and a mask. Having no time to change since his trip to the ocean, he tells everyone that it is too beautiful to throw trash into. Some goats arrive who might help with the garbage emergency, but they are so worn out they must take a nap. And anyway, only one of them speaks English, the other can only bleat. Out of options, King Friday and Lady Elaine Fairchilde take a purple jet to a cosmic television studio to appear on the talk show *The Universe Today*. King Friday would rather play his bass violin than talk about the garbage crisis, but he is interrupted by a stowaway factory worker Hilda Dingleboarder. Incredulously, he exclaims, "Oh, Mrs. Dingleboarder, do you know where you are?" We could all ask the same question as the cataclysmic narrative spins out surprising scenarios and gets downright weird.

Despite being a fantasy, the disaster in the Neighborhood of Make-Believe connects to real environmental issues. In fact, the "Caring for the Environment" series originally aired in April 1990, the week before the Sunday that Earth Day was set to go international. While he echoes apocalyptic themes, Rogers turns them on their head to attend to the needs and fragility of children. Instead of depicting the doom and destruction of the world, a view that might petrify children, Rogers speaks of a new world of helping and caring emerging. Rogers doesn't shy away from the severity of the issues but helps children imagine the world differently, a world they can enjoy, have hope for, and do something about. He wants a new creation from the love of, not the devastation of, the old one.

Rogers's apocalyptic environmentalism is not the popularized version found throughout culture. Popular apocalyptic stories often imagine an end to all things that is coming soon. Pollutants will render habitats toxic. Climate change will destroy the Earth and quite possibly everyone on it. People become diseased, they die, and they become savage or wild. The few who are saved find escape by going underground or flying into space. Life as we know it is over. There is only fear and terror, especially for children.

This kind of fear is already present in children today. In her essay "Children's Environmental Concerns," Susan Jean Strife calls it "ecophobia" and says children across the globe "express great anxiety over the state of the natural environment." Their anxiety comes from the children's sense of their future where natural forests and animal habitats are destroyed, the globe is rapidly warming, air pollution constricts breathing, and endangered animals die off quickly. The anxiety increases when they see images and hear stories about environmental disasters on screens. Not only is this bleak future coming, but the screens make it seem so big, overpowering, distant yet near, and incomprehensibly complex. Children then often want to withdraw from the problems. In her "How To Save the World and Other Lessons from Children's Environmental Literature," Clare Echterling says that when this doom-and-destruction type of environmentalism appears in children's stories, it feeds into children's anxiety. It paralyzes them. She finds that children avoid thinking about the environment and don't believe they can do anything to help. They despair. They become apathetic.

If you know Fred Rogers, you know he addresses fear but does not create it. He deals with issues to help children manage them. He does this even in his apocalyptic environmentalism. As a Presbyterian minister, Rogers draws on the biblical tradition of apocalypse. This version means to "reveal" or "uncover." It points to problems in the world but in a caring way to primarily attend to those who are suffering because of them. Images of the end of the world are less fire and brimstone and more a wiping away of tears, an end to sickness and sadness, and the making of all things new (Revelation 20:1–6). Biblical apocalypticism gives people new ways of seeing the world, hope that things will get better, and motivation to keep caring and acting. It is meant to inspire people to love and to keep loving even in difficult times. Addressing problems with comfort, hope, and love, it shouldn't be surprising that Rogers uses this apocalypticism to address environmental issues.

The Garbage Apocalypse

Rogers deliberately sequences episodes of "Caring for the Environment" to dramatize an ecological catastrophe building in the Neighborhood of Make-Believe. He begins with a local trash problem and quickly proceeds to picture a regional crisis, sketch global ruin, and imply impending galactic disaster. The Monday episode begins on garbage day, with Handyman Negri speaking with Trolley about how the amount of trash continues to increase. "Yes," Negri moans, surrounded by trash cans, "it seems to get more and more each year." In reply to Trolley's chimes, Negri exclaims, "I'm glad you don't," which seems to imply that Trolley has no garbage to throw away today.

Shortly thereafter, King Friday interrupts Handyman Negri's garbage collecting and asks Negri to play music with him. When Negri agrees, King Friday hands him a large stack of sheet music and says, "When I asked for two, the copier gave me 200. You'll just have to

Bob Dog describes King Friday and Handyman Negri's music as "Garbage Music" (episode 1616). Courtesy of the Fred Rogers Company.

throw the 198 away." Bob Dog, an actor in full costume who looks much like a large puppet, describes the music as "Garbage Music," qualifying it as "music beside the garbage," when King Friday is offended. While King Friday doesn't seem worried about the problem, the other neighbors begin to be. Mr. McFeely comes into the Neighborhood of Make-Believe to announce that the dump is full and offers to save King Friday's papers.

After his duet with the king, Handyman Negri heads over to the dump to see for himself. The dump is located in Someplace Else, the same part of town that includes Harriet Elizabeth Cow's school and Donkey Hodie's farm. Speaking with a rural accent, Harriet Cow informs Handyman Negri that the dump is full, so full in fact that they are building a fence to keep it from overflowing onto the farm and the school.

In his fantastical Neighborhood of Make-Believe, where King Friday does not think twice of sending his trash to Someplace Else,

Farmer Donkey Hodie and teacher Harriet Elizabeth Cow build a fence around the overflowing dump to protect the school (episode 1616). Courtesy of the Fred Rogers Company.

Rogers shows how society so often dumps its problems, including environmental ones, on areas where the poor live. Someplace Else is portrayed as an area of Appalachia, from Harriet Cow's accent to her dress to the hilly terrain. Not only is this the area where Fred Rogers is from—Southwest Pennsylvania is considered Northern Appalachia—Appalachia is home to historic environmental exploitation. The timber industry stripped the hillsides. The coal industry hollowed out the mountains. Now, the natural gas industry is destabilizing the land and poisoning the water. It is, and has been, what Rebecca Scott, author of *Removing Mountains*, calls a national sacrifice zone.

King Friday's lack of concern and the main characters' lack of awareness of the problem exposes a mindset that too often accompanies environmental problems. We could call it "toxic consciousness," to borrow a term from Cynthia Deitering. "Toxic consciousness" is a mindset that directs people's actions toward consumption, "pollution and waste." In the Neighborhood of Make-Believe, this mindset is accompanied by a general lack of awareness of what is occurring. It also enacts, to borrow another term but this one from Rob Nixon, a "slow violence." This is a situation where an environmental crisis unfolds "gradually and out of sight," often emerging so slowly that the violence is "typically not viewed as violence at all." If people have resources, they can protect themselves from these slowly building consequences and can even pretend like they aren't occurring. By contrast, the poor cannot, and so it is they who suffer first and the most. Meanwhile, most of society keeps going on, ignoring the problem and the suffering. Combined, "toxic consciousness" and "slow violence" explain why Donkey Hodie and Harriet Cow are already building a wall to save themselves and their land before anyone else even knows there is a trash problem!

Eventually, the main characters catch up and experience the fallout of the trash problem. On Tuesday's episode, everyone wears nose muffs, as their senses are overwhelmed with the stench. X the Owl complains, "I can't breathe with this thing on; please take it off!" The trash problem has become an air pollution problem. Along with environmental degradation, Southwestern Pennsylvania, particularly Pittsburgh where *Mister Rogers' Neighborhood* was filmed, suffered air pollution. In fact, shortly after a coal seam was discovered on the bank of its Monongahela River in 1762, Pittsburgh became known as "The Smoky City" or even "Hell with the Lid Off." By 1940, Pittsburgh was dark at all hours of the day. Rogers would have been familiar with this damning history as well as the city's cooperative effort with a successful and vibrant activist organization called GASP—Group Against Smog and Pollution. Founded in 1969, GASP helped Pittsburgh become a cleaner city and continues to advocate for clean air to this day. While we do not know if GASP inspired Rogers, it is hard not to imagine that he might echo their community efforts in Make-Believe's pollution and garbage crisis.

Lady Aberlin shows X the Owl her nose muff and they work together toward solutions to their garbage crisis (episode 1617). Courtesy of the Fred Rogers Company.

Rogers allows his characters to express anxiety in the face of overwhelming trash. He makes space in his episodes for discomfort and unease. He wants to affirm these feelings as valid, but he does not want to use them to paint a doom and gloom future. This space and these feelings are supposed to help us see the world more clearly. Instead of the blindness that can come from "toxic consciousness" and "slow violence," the feelings help us to recognize the problem and so see things from the perspective of those on the fringes. Rogers helps us to see not as King Friday does but as Harriet Cow does.

This approach, paying attention to those on the fringes, also comes from Rogers's faith. In his unpublished "Sermon for Installation of the Reverend Kenneth Barley," Rogers insists that God speaks from those on the margins. He writes, "How many times have you noticed that it's the little quiet moments in the midst of life which seem to give the rest extra-special meaning? God specializes in such things."

Rogers then proceeds to show how Jesus attended to voices on the margins and redefined kingship as serving these voices. It is no wonder that awareness of the garbage problem in the Neighborhood of Make-Believe comes from the voices of Somewhere-Else.

The result of such paying attention is to see ourselves as connected to others. The way trash threatens Harriet Cow's school establishes a clear connection between children who are familiar with school and those in Appalachia. As the people in the Neighborhood of Make-Believe start looking for a new dump, they investigate the communities around them. They find that Westwood's and Southwood's dumps are also full, so everyone has the same problem and so come together to seek a solution. In Thursday's episode, goats come down from Northwood. Even though they are exhausted when they arrive and immediately take a nap, Lady Aberlin knows they care about the problem, saying, "I know the goats could help us if they could just wake up," and proceeds to sing a wakeup song to them. Ironically, the goats are the most woken up to the problem and, although it is an emergency, they must take the time to care for themselves before they work out a collaborative solution. Of course, this also adds to the comfortable suspense. Rogers indulges anxiety while mitigating it in the (almost) patient confidence Lady Aberlin has in her goat neighbors. Even the mechanical Trolley is neighborly; it recognizes the crisis and expresses solidarity. When Trolley chimes, Lady Aberlin clearly understands, replying, "Thanks, Trolley, we need good luck with this garbage. It gets more and more every day." The garbage crisis continues to escalate, but everyone seems in it together.

Rogers emphasis on bringing people together is seen when Lady Elaine Fairchilde suggests asking *The Universe Today* for help with the trash cataclysm. Before Lady Aberlin understands that Lady Elaine means the intergalactic television program, Lady Aberlin remarks: "Oh, that's a good one. The whole universe should be mighty interested in this dilemma of ours." The impending doom seems so overwhelming that puppets are crying out to the heavens

Surrounded by small, overflowing trash cans, everyone is in it together: the Northwood goats, King Friday, Lady Aberlin, and Lady Elaine Fairchild, who seeks additional help on the cosmic television talk-show, *The Universe Today* (episode 1619). Courtesy of the Fred Rogers Company.

for help. Rogers suggests, through Lady Elaine, "We're going to find our solution on a television talk show!" This means of communication can connect everybody, locally and universally, to one another.

The conversations among citizens in Rogers's make-believe universe are vital to establishing neighborliness and dealing with real conflict. Matthew Ussia, in "Mister Rogers's Lessons for Democracy," explores how real communication about real problems in Rogers's pretend neighborhood contributes to a better, more just society. Ussia follows Junlei Li's point, made in the Morgan Neville's documentary *Won't You Be My Neighbor?*, that the Neighborhood of Make-Believe is a "space of conflict," by pointing out that this neighborhood is no "fantasy land," but a civic space. Rather than using magic, neighbors must work out their neighborhood problems together by building consensus, a primary lesson, Ussia argues, for people living in a democracy. He suggests that when individual citizens recognize and act on our mutual interdependency in a public space, it allows the private self and public face to most seamlessly coexist with others. This, Ussia argues, is "vital to our freedom" and is consistent with what a healthy democracy looks like. For Rogers, dialogue not only exposes the truth of our personal relationships but also the truth of our relationships with our environment, human, nonhuman, and material—be that useful objects and worn-out garbage.

The implicit belief is that these conversations and connections will move everyone to help solve the trash problem. In Wednesday's episode, Handyman Negri fans the trash's toxic fumes upward. Westwood's Mayor Maggie thanks him for the work that helps "for the time being," recognizing, as Handyman Negri does, that "it's anything but a permanent solution." Even so, he wants to help: "I might as well do something!" King Friday comes to recognize the problem and even pitches in by giving Handyman Negri a battery-powered fan. While this approach does not adequately address the scale of the garbage cataclysm, the neighbors continue to work together.

Rogers addresses the seriousness of environmental problems without frightening children. This is why he addresses the problems and the anxiety in the Neighborhood of Make-Believe more so than his television neighborhood. The Neighborhood of Make-Believe is a place where children can safely worry about problems, including environmental ones, in their own world. They will not become paralyzed with fear or give up in despair. Instead, they can follow along with the familiar characters to encounter the garbage problem and imagine a solution that works toward a new order, one of understanding and feeling, of hope and care, and of responsibility and love.

The New World Order

Rogers's story builds an imaginative world where everyone cares about all creatures. As he says in Thursday's episode, "Practically anything can happen in that Neighborhood of Make-Believe, but one thing is for sure, everyone is trying to help." On Friday, neighbors work together to find solutions to their disaster. Goats from Northwood call in to *The Universe Today* talk show to affirm that they will help separate the trash at the dumps all around the region. Hilda Dingleboarder, in her surprise appearance on the program, demonstrates how her newly invented machine for creative reuse will recycle what the goats recuperate. Watching these developments on their neighborhood television, characters in Make-Believe exclaim, "How natural!" as *The Universe Today* concludes. These actions are made possible by a new mindset, one that cares for the environment and all creatures, from their immediate and regional neighbors as well as those across the universe and in the ocean.

Rogers has built this world through imagination, by telling a story in the Neighborhood of Make-Believe. Writing about apocalyptic environmental literature, Timothy Gilmore maintains that ecological awareness is "inherently imaginative," requiring the wildness of the imagination to see the "unruly complexity" of what is real. When Lady Aberlin translates Old Goat's bleats, Rogers models how children can look to animals for unconventional ideas and sound strategies. When King Friday takes the Purple Jet into outer space, Rogers zooms out to the planetary implications of our actions. When Bob Dog makes trash into party hats, Rogers asks children to think about how celebrations can transform trash. Rogers insists that the Neighborhood of Make-Believe is not a daydream; it is intentionally using imagination to propel an awakening to reality. Rogers makes possible what Gilmore demands: "the need to think beyond a naïve reconnection with nature to our complex immersion within the wildness of ultimately uncontrollable systems, to endeavor to view the invisible through the imaginative capacity of ecological consciousness."

Rogers's apocalyptic story is meant to show a problem that is brewing, a problem that is causing trouble while also advancing a vision of a better world. Moreover, it is meant to highlight those who are suffering and the structures that enable that suffering so that a new, more just and caring world can come into being. Rogers's apocalyptic approach demands that his fantastical story is bound to the very real environmental crisis at hand. Rogers portrays attitudes and actions that are careless and exploitative, destructive first to the farm and school children, and then as a threat to everyone in the neighborhood and even the universe. Yet, he imagines this old world receding into the past, and the future world he projects becomes today's world. Rogers positions his pretend, better world as present, as happening. In the child's fantastically current and future world, people listen to animal wisdom, embrace technological innovation, and demand that everyone work together and do their part. The Neighborhood of Make-Believe citizens solve their crisis when the community comes together, something that cannot be accomplished without hope.

Fostering Hope

In envisioning this different, better world, the biblical apocalyptic tradition fosters hope by centering on God's love, a love that runs through all creatures. Rogers, without explicitly expressing his religious convictions in *Mister Rogers' Neighborhood*, echoes this hope in advancing a worldview whereby care is the connective tissue among individuals and communities. In his *Apocalyptic Ecology*, Micah Kiel argues that the coming apocalyptic "end" is a beginning, confident that evil "powers will fail, indeed the working of their downfall has begun." The biblical tradition always insists on hope because God's "entanglement" and "connectedness" with creation is absolute. God's deep love connects humanity and creation in a common destiny toward salvation. There is no room in the biblical tradition for failure. God becomes the center, not to do everything, but to sustain people, ensuring them that God is on their side working for the good of all of creation. Apocalyptic literature fosters hope because, whatever doom or destruction might be coming, whatever evil or cruelty is being done, God's love is working to overcome it. For Rogers, God's love is circulated in the love and care among people.

Despite the impending catastrophe in the Neighborhood of Make-Believe, the scenario always turns towards hope. Highlighting the garbage problem generates solutions and new possibilities. Throughout the story arc, people continually work on the garbage problem. Some solutions are impossible, some flawed, some wrongheaded, some would even further pollution, but, eventually, some work. The first round of solutions, which take up three of the five episodes, revolve around finding another dump. On Monday, Harriet Cow proposes this to Handyman Negri, who, after sharing it with Bob Dog, decides to take the idea to King Friday. King Friday tasks Lady Aberlin with finding another dump, and, on Tuesday, she asks X the Owl to fly around to find one. By Wednesday, Lady Elaine Fairchilde calls her friend Betty Okonak in Southwood. All of this frantic work fails. The characters in Neighborhood of Make-Believe come to know that Southwood and Westwood have the same problem. In fact, Southwood's situation is so bad it has declared a state of emergency. After pouring over a map of the region, it becomes painfully apparent that sending the trash to a local dump turns out to be impossible. However, everyone has begun talking and building a community of thinkers. Acknowledging the problem and spreading the word to look for solutions keeps neighbors hoping and thinking.

Rogers implies that solutions that simply move garbage around lack empathy and fail. For example, on Tuesday, Lady Elaine suggests that "we could put all of our garbage into an airplane and send it away ... [to] ... Just Anywhere." When Lady Aberlin notes that the people of Just Anywhere might not like it, Lady Elaine says, "I never thought of that." In the next episode, Lady Elaine proposes dumping the trash in the ocean, saying its big enough to hold anything, and Lady Aberlin notes that the fish might not like it. In this Wednesday episode, when everyone realizes that they must think beyond a geographical relocation, Rogers hints at mysterious sources of help. Rogers alerts neighbors that goats from Northwood will travel to the Neighborhood of Make-Believe to inspect the dump. In this pivotal episode, he also shows Mrs. Dingleboarder beginning work on a machine she is inventing which might help. In fact, a careful viewer might remember that Mrs. Dingleboarder mentioned the idea of recycling on Monday's episode, before the concept was fully explained and before Tuesday's trip to the recycling center.

In the face of overwhelming discouragement, Rogers embeds the beginnings of the real solution, still left to the imagination. These plot points enable Lady Aberlin to enthusiastically conclude, "We're all in this together!"—even during Wednesday's full-blown crisis. Ironically, Lady Elaine's terrible ideas generate a hopeful world. While neighbors do not give in to her proposals, they do not reprimand her. She is enabled to keep brainstorming. Finally, she hits upon her good idea on Thursday's episode, suggesting she appear on the talk show *The Universe Today* to ask others for help. Lady Elaine is undaunted when her own ideas are not enough and generously looks to others for new solutions. She embodies the hopeful attitude that the problem can and will be solved.

When Thursday's episode ends, there are no concrete solutions but two reasons to hope. Because neighbors have reached out to them, Old Goat and New Goat have arrived from Northwood, and they have specialized knowledge about garbage, their own dump being under control. Lady Elaine and King Friday are heading to the television studio of *The Universe Today*. In the last episode on Friday, the solutions come. Initially, viewers might think that goats were brought in to eat the trash. However, earlier in the episode, before traveling to the Neighborhood of Make-Believe, Mr. McFeely brought a live goat, named William, to Mister Rogers's television house. When Rogers says that he thought goats would eat anything, like cans and such, Mr. McFeely responds, "He [William the goat] doesn't eat just anything. That's not true. He likes nuts, and grains, and he likes vegetables [. . .] they're very particular about what they eat." This real-life moment lingers in the background when one sees the goats in the Neighborhood of Make-Believe. Undoing a particular stereotype and showing

Hilda Dingleboarder displays her recycling invention on the show *The Universe Today* (episode 1620). Courtesy of the Fred Rogers Company.

an unsurprising concern for animals since Rogers was a vegetarian, these puppet goats help the neighbors think in a new way. Highlighting communication, Old Goat and New Goat ask for a fax-machine to contact colleagues back in Northwood, who agree to send a team of goats to help "divide and conquer": divide up trash into different piles so that it can be recycled.

Alongside the Goats' plan, factory worker-turned-inventor Hilda Dingleboarder designs a recycling machine that creates new things out of old, thrown-away things. She shows it to everyone on *The Universe Today*. It turns out that intergalactic communication on broadcast television builds empathy and spreads awareness, but the technology is limited. It has propelled hope, but local neighbors have enacted the solutions. Summing up the goat and inventor achievements, Patrice, the host of the program, says, "So you see, folks, sometimes the solution to many problems can be found right next door." Rogers insists care is embedded in one's own community. Rogers's trip to a recycling center in an earlier episode may have helped children anticipate this solution, giving them hope and new ideas during the apocalyptic plot in the Neighborhood of Make-Believe.

Finding reserves of hope and solutions at home is particularly important for children. In "A Sense of Wonder: Cultivating an Ecological Identity in Young Children—and in Ourselves," Ann Pelo notes that parents do well when they employ wonder to foster concern about the environment. Parents inculcate wonder when they walk the land with children, teach them the names of things, help them explore the land with all of their senses, and create stories about it. Caring adults have the power to create a world of hope where problems can be overcome. In his 1990 pamphlet for caregivers, "Caring for Our Planet: Care That's Caught," produced in coordination with this week, Rogers nicely captures this idea. He describes an attitude that privileges hope:

> Even though caring for the environment can be hard for children to grasp, there's much we can offer them. The greatest thing they can learn from us is our attitude. When *we* turn off the lights and when *we* turn paper over to use the back of it, when *we* gather newspapers for recycling, and even when *we* marvel at a sunset, we send loud and clear messages to our children that caring for our planet is important to us. They'll take in those messages because children want to be like the important adults in their lives.

Rogers's message here turns between adults and children, offering hope for the whole family.

If children are to hope and not despair, they need to see people working to resolve the problem and know that solutions are possible. In his commencement address for Saint Vincent College in 2000, one of his few public talks on religion, Rogers articulates the importance of others in providing hope. In his talk he states that "we just don't get to be competent human beings without many different investments from others." He then takes a moment of silence and asks everyone to think of those people "who nourish you at the deepest part of your being . . . anyone who has ever loved you and wanted what was best for you in life." According to Rogers, what gives us hope in the world are these people as well as their care for us and our thanks for their gifts. They enable you "to feel for others," "to appreciate your life," and "to bow to your neighbor in that sacred space between grateful hearts." Rogers puts the responsibility on all of us to "nourish" others in the deepest part of their being, and implicit in the background is his own hope, the apocalyptic hope, that God's love for the poor and suffering is operative in the universe to right wrongs. For Rogers, that love becomes our love, and we can act on it.

Embodying Actions

Fostering hope while imagining a new order empowers people to act. As Robin Veldman notes in his "Narrating the Environmental Apocalypse," the biblical apocalyptic tradition embeds motivation within its stories by offering a "warning that humans can prevent catastrophe, but only if they act soon, and decisively." Biblical apocalyptic literature offers a way forward in promoting actions that cooperate with God's work in bringing about a new, more just, social order. Rogers uses his apocalyptic vision inside the Neighborhood of Make-Believe to imagine a new order and see hope in the actions of others, but he steps outside Make-Believe to depict actions for children.

When Rogers returns to his television neighborhood, he provides examples of recycling activities that enable children to bring the environmental story of the Neighborhood of Make-Believe into their lives. These mainly take the form of crafts created by recycling household materials. Rogers enacts how to make postcards with leftover materials, a tree out of toilet paper tubes, and a bird feeder from an old milk carton. He furthers this creativity by exploring how recycled objects can be put together in more complex ways. He makes a game out of an old paper bag and some balls by trying to roll the balls into the bag. He shows how to make a cardboard box look like a television set, using bottle caps for knobs, how to make puppets from balls, pens, and handkerchiefs, and how to put the two together to put on a television show.

Beyond regular recycling, Rogers offers conceptual recycling activities. He repeatedly reminds viewers to think if something can be reused or recycled before throwing it away. In this way, he values imagination as a key to recycling as it helps people think of ways to reuse something. At least twice, he likens memory to recycling because it is a way for people to use their past again and again. To emphasize this point on memory, on Wednesday, Rogers uses a clip from an earlier, 1972, program where Mr. McFeely's wife reuses household things. Mrs. McFeely makes a bird feeder from a milk carton, implying that what feeds humans can also feed animals, and vice-versa as Rogers takes a taste of the crackers and peanut butter inside! She shows him a pillow made from torn sheets, suggesting that recycled consumer goods can give comfort over and over again. Finally, she shows Rogers a rug by her entry door and explains how her friends made this rug from old wool clothes. Here, she implies that we dress ourselves and beautify our spaces with color and memories. She states that these efforts, while laborious, are worthy: "There are lot of things you can do with old things, but you have to take the time to make it."

Reflecting on the past visit with Mrs. McFeely, Rogers remarks, "I like to remember times like that. In fact, memories are things that you can use over and over again. It's good to have memories that don't wear out, no matter how much you think about them." In addition to thinking of reusing memories, Rogers proves to children that their big ideas and small actions are valuable. All of Mrs. McFeely's remade objects come from household materials and are reconstituted within the home. Rogers domesticates reusing to bring the lesson home for the child. There is work to do to care for the environment, and children can do that work right at home. In fact, they do it when they play.

In "To Know, To Decide, To Act," Glynne Mackey states that children become overwhelmed if they cannot act. While parents and

Recalling a memory from a 1972 episode (episode 1205), Rogers examines a bird feeder that Mrs. McFeely made from a milk carton (episode 1618). Courtesy of the Fred Rogers Company.

teachers should not overburden children with too much responsibility, these authority figures also have a responsibility to develop a child's agency, so they can grow into a caring and active member of the community. In fact, J. Joy James and Robert Bixler argue in "Children's Role in Meaning Making Through Their Participation in an Environmental Education Program" that the choices of children are key to connecting with the environment and developing a concern about it. Likewise, Susan Jean Strife's research found that children "feel better about the state of the environment if they are given more opportunities to engage and participate in environmental stewardship and civic responsibility." In other words, environmental activism relies on reinforcements between hope and action, which propel each other.

For children, and perhaps for most of us, actions need not and often cannot be large-scale. Instead, activities like working on a flower or vegetable garden, participating in a recycling program, or contributing to a schoolwide composting program promote both hope and further action. For the very young, Rogers's recommendation to make one's own toys and sorting recyclables is heartwarming and practical. Such small tasks can foster children's sense of agency and set them on a lifelong path of environmental concern through "incremental responsibility." Rogers's "Caring for the Environment" series shows adults, grown-up puppets, and adult Old and New Goat puppets leading the community toward solutions, releasing children from guilt and primary responsibility. Simultaneously, Rogers shows children what care they can give, to pets and to toys, which help children move from imagination and hope to action.

Apocalyptic Reality

Rogers himself creatively recycled and revised his own ideas and tactics as his television program developed. By the 1990 "Caring for the Environment" week, he expertly controls each aspect of his program. His flashback to the memory with Mrs. McFeely reveals how Rogers changes his own ideas around pretend play and furthered the apocalyptic values that connect imaginative reckoning with changing reality. This flashback scene comes from a Friday episode in 1972, eighteen years earlier. Rogers himself is clearly younger, and embedding this 1972 scene into his 1990 program is as authentic as it is productive. While there were not yet themed weeks in 1972, this episode and the one before it can be seen as a precursor to the "Caring for the Environment" series. The messages around reusing household goods are consistently portrayed in the television neighborhood. However, the lessons around caring for the environment that occur in the Neighborhood of Make-Believe vary from Rogers's 1990 lessons.

In the 1972 Thursday and Friday episodes in Neighborhood of Make-Believe, Cornflake S. Pecially's factory has polluted the creek with wood dye which has impacted the factory's own water wheel

In the same 1972 episode, Lady Elaine's magic boomerang cleans up the pollution in the Neighborhood of Make-Believe (episode 1205). Courtesy of the Fred Rogers Company.

and King Friday's waterfall. Like the 1990 episodes, initial efforts to remove or clean the pollution are thwarted, but people continue to communicate and work together. Eventually Lady Elaine comes to the rescue with her magic boomerang, making the stain magically go back into its can. Cornflake S. Pecially, seeing a dirt stain on Robert Troll's hands, realizes that he can use organic dye made from the earth that will not pollute their neighborhood waterways. They recognize this approach as indigenous, Cornflake S. Pecially remarks, "Sure, the Indians knew so many things that we need to learn all over again."

While Rogers offers a solution to future pollution that asks children to think in new ways, he is unable to imagine a real solution to current pollution. Back in the television neighborhood, Rogers snaps while remarking, "Boomerang, Toomerang, Zoomerang! Doesn't happen like that in our neighborhood. No, we don't do things by magic here, just in Make-Believe. When we need to clean something up in our neighborhood, we do it ourselves." Here, instead of looking directly at the camera, one of the key ways Rogers intimately connects to his television neighbors, he shakes his head and looks away from the camera. He seems to realize that he has not offered a real solution to a real problem but merely a pretend one in a make-believe neighborhood.

In the coming years, and certainly during the themed weeks that began in 1979 and persisted until his last episodes in 2001, Rogers develops his connections between make-believe and reality. As Susan Larkin notices in "Fantasy as Free Space: Mister Rogers' Neighborhoods," the real world of Mister Rogers's television neighborhood isn't so real; it's idyllic, populated by kind adults who are invariably thoughtful and caring. It is the pretend world in the Neighborhood of Make-Believe that might feel more real; this is where conflicts are played out. This is where people and puppets may say hurtful things and act mean and throw tantrums. Larkin calls Rogers's fantasy space a "free space:" "To Rogers, fantasy is not about mysticism; fantasy is a free space to try things out. The space is freeing because it is safe and because it is unhampered by many society constraints or expectations."

Rogers uses the Neighborhood of Make-Believe to challenge children to "think carefully, thoughtfully, and often outside of established patterns within a protected space." Rogers consistently uses imaginative play to turn toward new ways of thinking, such as considering what animals would do or say to save the environment from being overrun by trash. And that play is always tightly bound to the concerns in his television world and tuned in to the young child's social and emotional development. Rogers's apocalypticism opens minds and promotes a hopeful and caring future, working toward making reality less like the Neighborhood of Make-Believe and more like Mister Rogers's neighborhood.

Chapter Two

The Art of Environmentalism
Integral Ecology in Fred Rogers's Neighborhoods

The opening segment of "Caring for the Environment" depicts Mister Rogers comfortably and routinely at home, showing the viewers a greeting card that he received from a friend. He displays the pretty fish on the front and shows the message inside the card. He asks children if they receive greeting cards or know anyone who does. Rogers explains, "I'm interested to know what people do with greeting cards when they do get them. I'm sorry to say a lot of people just throw them away. But some people make scrapbooks of them, collect them, and save them. Other people turn them into other greeting cards so they can use them again. I'll show you what I mean." As Rogers walks to the kitchen table, he pauses to show his aquarium fish the drawing of the fish on the card, implying that art objects and real-life creatures are connected. At the table, he displays how, with a little tape, the envelope can be refolded and reused. He tears the card in half to demonstrate how the picture can be mailed again as a post card.

The card and message are both important. The greeting card is a powerful choice for Rogers's recycling theme. His reused stationary can be mailed to recirculate the good feeling it brought him. Reusing

Rogers begins the series by reusing a greeting card (episode 1616). Courtesy of the Fred Rogers Company.

the envelope brings to light Rogers's emphasis on the value of the inside. Rogers literally turns the envelope inside out to reveal that this space is ready for addressing. The message is also important. It is a child's thoughts and feelings which should be first engaged before acting—whether making art, reusing scrap paper, or composing a thank you note. The picture on the card itself—a drawing of a fish—ties caring for the self and the sender with caring for the environment and its creatures. The point of this opening is taken up again when Rogers visits the coral reef in Thursday's episode, which is the experience that occasioned his friend to send the card.

In "Caring for the Environment," Rogers celebrates art as a process for reusing and recycling. He shows his audience the power we have to transform what might be trash into meaningful expressions of care. Rogers suggests that art can open up one's imagination to envision a system of circulating love made up of caring relationships through space and time.

Rogers spoke about how artistic expression fulfills the very goals of education in his "Encouraging Creativity" commencement address at Thiel College in 1969. He explained how important and natural it is for children, and adults, too, to make and study art to express their inner uniqueness, perspectives, and selves. Allowing children to know themselves in this expressive way has the power to "increase their feelings of personal worth, responsibility, and freedom." Rogers associates artistic process and products with campaigns for global peace asking, "Isn't it possible that we in America have underestimated the role of the creative artist in international affairs?"

David Boersema recognizes Rogers's philosophy of art as serving both the self and the civic body. Boersema argues that Rogers's philosophy of art, while connected to his environmentalism, is broader in emphasis. He discusses how "Rogers consciously and intentionally used what he saw as the virtues of the arts in his goal of helping children become fulfilled and virtuous persons." Boersema argues that Rogers's emphasis on artwork as both process and product allows children to act and make change; namely, creating art connects children to others and propels personal transformation. Referencing Rogers's use of the song "Tree Tree Tree," which we discuss in chapter five as a work of performance art, Boersema asserts that Rogers uses art as a tool for social activism. Here, Boersema's attention to Rogers's environmentalism revolves around appreciation, importance, value, and care of the nonhuman, or nature. Art helps children know what they think and feel, as well as communicate to others in order to build community and change people's attitudes and behaviors. In short, Boersema shows how Rogers's philosophy around art can help the creator and the viewer become more virtuous. Through contemplating and creating art, Rogers helps children understand their connection to nature and deepen as well as act on their environmental imagination. Ultimately, for Boersema, Rogers's use of art was meant "to help us (make us?) see the world differently, and maybe even be a means of social and political activism."

Leo Sewell's bricolage sculptures (episode 1618). Courtesy of the Fred Rogers Company.

Mister Rogers's Television Neighborhood: Turning Places Inside Out

What is the relationship between art and real life? What are the relationships between this drawing of a fish, the pet fish in Rogers's tank, and the fish in the coral reefs? How can art help people imagine and come to know a larger, connected world? How can creating art foster meaningful relationships in real life? Rogers explores these questions in the middle three episodes of the series through various field trips to a recycling center, artist studio, and ocean habitat.

Rogers emphasizes the power of art in Wednesday's episode when Mr. McFeely brings a home video showing his visit to sculptor Leo Sewell's studio. Sewell uses recycled objects to fashion bricolage artwork. Emphasizing the mental work required for artistic creation, Rogers exclaims, "a lot of thought goes into that work" as Mr. McFeely explores drawers and shelves, looking at the raw material Sewell uses for his sculptures. The incredible number of drawers echoes the configuration of a puzzle box with nested drawers which he displayed at the start of the episode. Sewell's compartments, however, are full. He has filled them with salvaged refuse, echoing the

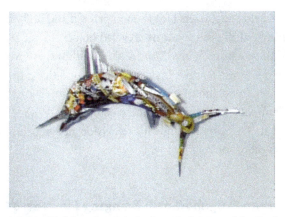

Leo Sewell's fish sculpture (episode 1618). Courtesy of the Fred Rogers Company.

imperative of the recycling center field trip the episode before. The artist proves that there is a place for everything; everything can be saved, reused, and given a meaningful existence with thoughtfulness, patience, and creativity. What might look like chaos and trash in the outside world, Sewell has thoughtfully organized and reshaped into playful, joyful sculptures.

In the studio, Mr. McFeely points out a large sculpture of a marlin, and this artwork links up with the greeting card and the fish in Mister Rogers's aquarium to prepare for Thursday's field trip, which will be a memory about a visit to the coral reef. Just as Rogers does not show people throwing away objects, Rogers does not throw away memories. Instead of turning things into trash after they are used, Rogers's reuse makes connections by recycling memories, ideas, and objects, and associating them.

Rogers illustrates how the imagination can reveal the real world when he plays peekaboo at the end of Wednesday's episode and the beginning of Thursday's episode. Having linked the two episodes, Rogers explains that he wants to share with his audience the memory of going to visit oceanographer Sylvia Earle and seeing the fish in the coral reef.

In this field trip, Rogers builds upon printed and sculptural representations of the fish made of recycled objects to get at the real fish and their natural home. More and more things are connected, from their outside to their inside and from one thing to another. Rogers builds a neighborhood with countless connections between people, animals, and places. He doesn't stop there. With the trip to the coral reef, Rogers expands his television neighborhood to an ocean neighborhood.

The Ocean Neighborhood: Bringing Elsewhere Close

In "Snorkeling with Sylvia Earle," on Thursday's episode, Rogers visits Laguna Reef, Florida, snorkels, and discusses fish and their ocean home with scientist Sylvia Earle. First, Rogers boards the *Infante*, a clear reference to the cognate infant. They talk about Earle's childhood interest in the ocean and her vacations to the beach.

Earle makes direct comparisons between fish and children, saying that all "young things" are "curious." Here, Rogers and Earle propose that fish have dignity, that they have feelings that accompany their behaviors propelling them beyond instinct. They suggest that for the fish and for the child to be healthy, they must be cared for. Both are vulnerable, so both need protection. This care is emotional and physical. Fish and child should be respected and protected from pollution. These values reverberate in the Neighborhood of Make-Believe when Lady Aberlin and other adults tell Lady Elaine Fairchilde that the fish would not like it if they dumped the trash in the ocean.

Next, Rogers and Earle swim among the fish in the reef. It is a meditative swim, accompanied by music, and celebrates the beauty of the coral reef. Rogers's viewers take in the habitat and fish. It is almost like a piece of performance art, where the movements of fish are followed, no words are spoken, while Johnny Costa plays improvisational piano music. This moment stands out, creating a memory that the child viewer can return to, like the memories of

Rogers joins Sylvia Earle on a snorkeling expedition (episode 1619). Courtesy of the Fred Rogers Company.

Sylvia Earle's family vacations or Mister Rogers's memory of this very experience that this video represents.

Rogers's short underwater film encourages children to develop an ecological imagination. In "Beyond Fluidity: A Cultural History of Cinema Under Water," Nicole Starosielski suggests that successful marine environmentalism can be advanced when films "frame the aquatic landscape as our neighborhood." Her use of Rogers's signature term for place imbues the ocean with lively neighbors and civic dramas. After the swim, Rogers and Earle remark that they are grateful for their friendship and for becoming friends with the fish. Familiarity has propelled neighborliness. Becoming neighbors has advanced good feelings, feelings of connection and gratitude. In fact, when Rogers emerges from his underwater viewing of the reef, he declares it is "a beautiful day in this neighborhood!" Starosielski, like Rogers, advocates the portrayal of ocean ecosystems as "a social space, a territory over which inequality continues to circulate." Rogers explains this inequality to children by highlighting how vulnerable fish are because water is their home, so, as he says several times in this episode, it is no place for trash.

When the piano music and ocean imagery fade out, the viewers come back to Rogers, who has been relishing his memory as he shared it. He is still sitting on his bench and has traded his scuba flippers for sneakers. Rogers then shows viewers pictures of three different types of angelfish. He clarifies, "all three are angelfish and all three are different." These photographs represent the very real fish children saw Rogers swimming with and focuses on the dignity of each fish and the importance of caring for wildlife. Rogers pauses over these fish photographs, in his slow and quiet style. These pictures act much like the art Jessica Whitelaw studies in "disquieting picture books." Whitelaw sees pictures as art forms that "invite close looking." Teachers and parents, like Rogers, can position pictures as moments for "embracing (ambiguity), opening (to hurt), pausing (for interruption), witnessing (resistance), and hearing (silences)." Rogers's nature photographs of angelfish give children a moment to consider the silence of the fish, wonder how fish and children are similar, and hint that hurting fish hurts people.

Rogers photographs reveal another way that art forges connections. The reality of these photographs is important. Rogers explains, "It's a whole, beautiful, real world out there under the sea." The photographs of fish are a placeholder for some real thing that is absent. They show the diversity of angelfish to work toward an understanding of creatures. The photographs are realistic images of these fish, yet Rogers has them do more than simply show what fish look like. Rogers's uses these pictures to remind the viewer of the coral reef excursion, activating the wonder of that experience and driving empathy toward vulnerable, silent fish. Thus, the photographs do not solely depict the outside, physical world but also point to a world of relationships and care that was experienced in snorkeling.

With the photographs, Rogers celebrates the differences and similarities among fish, and between fish and children,

Integral Ecology in Rogers's Neighborhoods

Rogers shows photographic art of angelfish (episode 1619). Courtesy of the Fred Rogers Company.

implying that each and every creature is different and unique. Even as we all have the same sort of feelings and needs, Rogers assures his viewers that we all express ourselves differently and that specialness is nourishing. All animals belong to communities, what scientists might call species, but they are all different. Rogers locates that uniqueness where it is easy to see: on the body.

Still at the fish tank, Rogers sings "Everybody's Fancy" after feeding his fish. The song insists that all bodies are unique and each one has dignity, requiring respect and care. He moves from the other to the child's self to Rogers himself: "Some are fancy on the outside. Some are fancy on the inside. Everybody's fancy. Everybody's fine. Your body's fancy and so is mine." Rogers follows his charming song by reinforcing its lessons, explaining, "There is something fancy about every creature in our world and something fine about us too. Each person. Each fish. Each animal. Each bird. Each living creature. The important thing for us is to look for what's fine in everybody and that will help us to want to take care of everybody and give us a really good feeling." Rogers implies that everyone has dignity, and, when we see it, we will want to honor it.

Rogers sings "Everybody's Fancy" after he feeds his fish (episode 1619). Courtesy of the Fred Rogers Company.

Later in the episode, Rogers shows just how close these faraway places and creatures might be. Directly after viewing the angelfish photographs, Rogers proceeds to feed his aquarium fish, and the camera zooms in on the angelfish in his own tank. He exclaims, "Beautiful creatures! These fish live in the water; their home is *this* water. If you were a fish, you wouldn't want someone dumping garbage in your home. Nobody would want that." Rogers instructs children to imagine themselves as fish, building empathy, and exposing the universal need for a clean home.

Not only are different creatures and homes worth respecting, they are also talked about as connected. As Earle explains, "The ocean is vital to the good health of the planet. So much of the oxygen we breathe is generated in the ocean by the plants that live there. And it's part of just good common sense to take care of this ocean that, in its way, takes care of all of us." Rogers and Earle hope their television viewers can somehow see the invisible air we breathe and recognize the clear water as home. Rogers wants his viewers to see the coral reef as interdependent with their own neighborhood and bodies.

Rogers's Integral Ecology

Through the art and the visit to the coral reef, Rogers dignifies each individual creature and habitat and brings a connected world into sharper focus. Pictures of angelfish, angelfish swimming with Rogers and Earle, and the angelfish in Rogers's house are related. A picture of a fish is coupled with Rogers's fish. A bricolage marlin is allied with recycling. Coral reefs and family rooms, aquariums and houses, ocean and air swim back and forth between each other. All kinds of connections are seen, bringing together the outside and the inside, the near and the far, the past and the present. Rogers uses art to help see a meaningfully interconnected world where everything and everyone is valuable.

Rogers's gentle associations might reveal a deeper significance. It is probably not a coincidence that what connects things are artistic images of fish. Because Christians used the Greek word for fish (*ichthys*) as an acronym for "Jesus Christ, Son of God, Savior," and because Jesus associated with fishermen and fed people with fish, Christians often used a fish symbol to identify themselves. For Christians, Jesus links invisible, spiritual realities and visible, physical realities, as Christians believe that the invisible God becomes visible in the person of Jesus (Col 1:15–20). It is in a similar move to suggest, as does Carol Zaleski, that Rogers's art can be considered "sacred art." Sacred art uses religious inspiration and motifs to uplift the mind to spiritual realizations. In "Caring for the Environment," Rogers uses fish art to dramatize that all creation has inherent value and all creation is connected. Chris Buczinsky asserts as much when articulating Rogers's "environmental ethics," which "ties our treatment of the earth back to the way we conceive of individuals." Buczinsky sums it up this way: "the best way to stop polluting our environment, Mister Rogers says, is to realize that every individual is special, a creature of God's creation."

Rogers's environmental ethics are a part of his ecological consciousness, a broader perspective which forecasts and resonates with the idea of "integral ecology," a term used by Pope Francis in his 2015 encyclical *Laudato Sí: On Care for Our Common Home*. The word "integral" means essential or fundamental, something necessary to make something complete. Integral also implies relationality, something networked together and mutually intertwined. And integral ecology, most basically, means that every single part—each person, animal, bug, and thing—are meaningfully related to the whole ecological world, physical and spiritual. Pope Francis asks that believers "recognize the ecological commitments which stem from our convictions" suggesting that justice demands care for self, others, God, and Earth.

Like Rogers, Francis notes that art is essential for helping us to see these connections. Too often, economic desires dominate the way people think and act. This narrow mindset that thinks everything is to be consumed reduces the natural world to resources ready for use and ripe for exploitation. For Francis, beauty "manages to overcome reductionism through a kind of salvation" by liberating people from this narrow view of the world. Art can free people from throwaway culture by propelling the imagination to recognize the truth of connection, the joy of interdependence, and the gratification of engaging in responsible actions. Creating and witnessing art nourishes a spiritual and tangible connection to creation, defining our relationships with things and others through care rather than use.

In "Caring for the Environment," Rogers hints that failing to see integral connections can be dangerous, implying, in particular, that polluting the ocean harms fish and people who cannot breathe easily without this healthy ecosystem. While maintaining that water is home to all sorts of aquatic life, Rogers and Earle insist that is also necessary for human life, so much so that many consider it a right. Yet, if disconnected from these lives, water can be exploited in economic calculations. While the threat to the ocean in the Neighborhood of Make-Believe is minimized and discarded, real-life analogues abound. Companies like Freedom Industries leaked chemical waste into the Elk River in 2014, polluting the water of

300,000 people in West Virginia. Or, in the same year, the city of Flint, Michigan, changed its water supply without adequate resources to treat it in order to save money. It left the city without clean water. These incidents and others like them show how those who polluted the water did not value its connections to their human or aquatic neighbors and how all creatures suffered. Rogers uses art to help children keep in mind how water ecosystems that they cannot see have a real impact on many lives.

To undervalue water is not just to deny its physical necessity, even its potential status as a human right, but also its spiritual dimension. In the Christian tradition, the Water of Life is the Holy Spirit that imbues all of creation with God's love. In a similar way, Rogers demonstrates that the watery worlds are close at hand and connected to the health of every neighborhood. Rogers employs art to reveal and memorialize the connections between neighborhoods and creatures who call those places home. He uses art to dramatize both why and how we care.

The Neighborhood of Make-Believe: Creating the Future's Past

In Thursday's trip to the coral reef, Rogers asks Earle outright: "What can we do to take care of places like this, these seas of ours?" Earle outlines three ways to work toward environmental activism: cultivating awareness of ocean habitats, recognizing interdependence between ecosystems, and, simply "minding our manners" to be friendly with other animals and respectful of other neighborhoods. As a television program for family viewing, Rogers proposes small but worthy actions, asking children to reuse scraps to make art and grown-ups to drive their glass, cans, and cardboard to the recycling center. He also holds up people, like Cindy, who swam with Rogers and Earle. These activists who care for the fish, the animals, and our planet, and who thereby make the world "safe" for everyone, are his "heroes." They help viewers imagine themselves as, and perhaps one day become, people with the power to be activists like Earle and Rogers advocate. They can practice, for Rogers, an ethic of care that sees the family as extending from the domestic home to ever-widening neighborhoods.

While children can see the connections between neighborhoods and homes, Rogers does not expect them to act outside of their own. He does not pressure them to become activists as preschoolers and tackle the difficult problems facing the environment. Instead, he is forming them to become caring people, supporting the foundation for an adult life where their values and compassion can then be put into action. Still, he equips children with small actions they can take to live out their caring feelings.

Rogers emphasizes these small actions in his trips to the Neighborhood of Make-Believe. Rogers explores how little trash items can and will fill the deep insides of huge dumps and how imaginative, fantastic play can be acted on in the real, outside world. As explored in chapter one, as the Neighborhood of Make-Believe's garbage crisis unfolds, the regions' dumps are found overflowing and trash closes in on public spaces. The neighborhood's own dump is in a place on the edge of the neighborhood called Someplace Else. It is also where the farm and school are located. Here, Rogers alludes to the school of fish viewers visited in the last episode, connecting fish and children, who have no real power over the destruction of their homes.

When Rogers implies that fish and children have things in common, when he states that they are "both curious" he makes space for the threatening idea that if people do not care about fish then they might not care about children. The Neighborhood of Make-Believe is an imaginary space where children can actively and openly worry about these troubling ideas that are hinted at in Mister Rogers's neighborhood. In Make-Believe, protective adults—the real-life actors in the Neighborhood of Make-Believe—mitigate the child's (and the fish's) powerlessness. When puppet Lady Elaine Fairchilde proposes throwing trash in the ocean, echoing what companies in the real world do in dumping their waste into rivers, she is immediately told that the fish would not like it.

While the caring adults in Make-Believe work together to try to solve the garbage crisis, Rogers's puppets save the day. As chapter one asserts, Rogers's puppets reveal an interconnected world where everyone comes together to solve a problem. What becomes clear in Thursday's episode is that the goats and the Dingleboarder machine mimic the strategies artist Leo Sewell has used to create his art. The puppet goats from Northwood will sort the trash, sending what can be recycled to puppet Hilda Dingleboarder's newly invented machine for creative reuse. Children, too, can sort recyclables and hunt through paper scraps and sewing boxes for redeemable items they can refashion into artistic crafts.

Hilda Dingleboarder's machine makes two things on *The Universe Today*, both of which would be simple crafts children could make. First, Hilda instructs Patrice to process a crumpled-up piece of paper, which the machine turns into a fan. This object may remind the viewer of the fanning Handyman Negri had been doing in Make-Believe to try to disperse the piled-up garbage's overwhelming smell. Hilda's machine makes trash into something that helps the neighbors deal with trash.

Next, Patrice puts the fan in Hilda's machine, which turns it into a strip of paper crowns. Children, too, could make and decorate paper crowns. King Friday, also Patrice's guest on the talk show, enthusiastically approves. He has had a remarkable change of heart, attitude, and practice, the same conversion Rogers might hope for in his television viewers. On Monday, King Friday wastefully photocopies extra sheets of music, making 200 instead of two copies, and says they'll just have to be thrown away. Ironically, King Friday's irresponsible musical art has had a wasteful byproduct, which, thankfully, Mr. McFeely arrives to save, taking the paper from a bewildered Handyman Negri.

By Friday, though, King Friday takes the right attitude toward his musical performances, largely because of a transformation

Hilda Dingleboarder shows how artistic projects can advance recycling efforts, presenting a fan and then crown to King Friday and Patrice, the host of *The Universe Today* (episode 1620). Courtesy of the Fred Rogers Company.

in how technology is used. Rather than misusing a photocopier machine, Patrice, the host of the cosmic television program *The Universe Today* uses television productively. She employs mass media to gather ideas and comments to solve the environmental disaster. When the solutions to their problem emerges, King Friday announces that he will play his bass violin. This ephemeral performance he calls "Universal Gratitude," and the celebration has no waste and extends out to the galaxy.

King Friday becomes an example of just the kind of person who receives help and becomes grateful for it. Children can then be like King Friday—even wearing crowns like those produced by Hilda's recycling machine! Just as King Friday is connected to the people in his Neighborhood and the Neighborhood of Make-Believe is connected to all the communities around it, children can play at being their own king by promising to grow up open-minded

King Friday's "Universal Gratitude" song debuted on *The Universe Today* (episode 1620). Courtesy of the Fred Rogers Company.

and open-hearted like the powerful King Friday. Playing at being in charge, children can contemplate the extent of their kingdom and how it connects with other people and neighborhoods. The Neighborhood of Make-Believe becomes a place where children's crafts and homemade toys become artwork, and, as art, express and fortify their own values and draw children into other worlds and into relationships with other people.

In this final episode's segment, returning to Mister Rogers's neighborhood, Rogers echoes this kind of artistic play by showing his viewers how to take household objects and turn them into puppets. Rogers creates a drama for them and has them sing a song that celebrates their differences yet allows them to collaborate and sing together. It is imaginative play that, for Rogers, is a form of recycling. Children reimagine objects and so reimagine the world, expanding it into new neighborhoods, including new people, and solving new problems. The artistic play fosters an understanding of the world where everything is connected. It sets the foundation for children to recycle and care for the environment.

Rogers ends this final episode of the week with his song "I'm Proud of You." Along with King Friday's "Universal Gratitude," the songs work together, celebrating musical art as environmental activism. Rogers drives the point home when talking about the song in a message for his young and adult viewers: "When you feel proud about who you are growing to be, then you can feel proud about who your friends and your neighbors are growing to be. That's a good feeling: when you can feel proud about somebody else." Rogers suggests that the relationships among neighbors and creatures, as well as the relationship we have with ourselves, can increase our capacity for care and work toward environmental activism.

Rogers's closing remarks echo the message on the greeting card that began the series, which included a note of thanks from producer Margy Whitmer, "I can't tell you what a pleasure it was to spend time with you and your friends snorkeling [. . .] I am grateful for that very special experience." The week of "Caring for the Environment" episodes works toward acknowledging an appreciation and gratitude for our neighbors and neighborhoods. Rogers imagines the Neighborhood of Make-Believe's present, particularly the revolution in thinking and acting that unfolds during this week's series, as a better future's past. Rogers imagines what we would have to have done to create the world we want to live in, and he gives thanks to us all in advance.

Art Works

Rogers's integral ecology uses art to expose the connection between everything and the reason why we should care for all things, so it is unsurprising that he imbues every aspect of his television program with art. The program is something that can sharpen our ability to see the connections between all the neighborhoods in our world, both human and animal. Rogers maintains that children's media is more than a commodity, a throwaway half-hour that is quickly consumed, forgotten, and then trashed. By his lights, children's programs should instead help us to see ourselves in relationship to others, to be kind to neighbors (human and aquatic) and so build neighborhoods of care. Kathy Merlock Jackson ties Rogers's "prosocial values" to his broader mission of "social responsibility," finding in the medium of television itself the key to Rogers's "social justice mission." His use of art and his transformation of his television program to art both heed this call.

As Jane Bennett says of literary text, Rogers's children's television program is a kind of art that "might help us live more sustainably, with less violence toward a variety of other bodies." The program itself—in its layered stories, songs and music, field trips, home videos, art projects, intimate conversations with Mister Rogers, and episodic structure that reiterates and develops habits of mind and heart—works to make the invisible tangible and real. *Mister Rogers' Neighborhood* is like the poetry Bennett praises because it opens our eyes, extending us beyond ourselves to recognize connections and relationships. She explains that "[poetry] can help us feel more of the liveliness hidden in such things [like trash and household objects] and reveal more of the threads of connection binding our fate to theirs." Rogers explores how the fate of trash is the fate of our neighborhoods and is the fate of our families and ourselves.

Rogers uses art to helps us see our neighborhood as a place connected to other neighborhoods and enveloped in a mutual dependency and cherished beauty. Creating and appreciating art empowers children, concentrating on their inner lives and using their values to act in the world. Art can remind us that what we might think is trash can usually be reused or recycled. Taking care of trash can be a playful and transformative celebration of the world, the creatures in it, and our very selves.

Chapter Three

Puppets and Animal Wisdom
Ecological Conversion

In the Neighborhood of Make-Believe, live actors, actors in animal costumes, animal puppets, and humanoid puppets all live as neighbors. Rogers imagines how animals contribute to our world. He anthropomorphizes them while working toward an ecological imagination that sees in each animal its own worth and perspective. He uses puppet animals to question our assumptions, sometimes startling us into an appreciation of animal wisdom. The way Rogers engages understanding and empathizing about animals can be captured by the traditional Christian term of conversion, which means, in essence, a change of heart. A conversion experience enables a kind of turning around and changing direction in one's perspective, attitude, behavior, or even life. Rogers uses his Neighborhood of Make-Believe to enact these changed perspectives, particularly around the goats who help with the trash catastrophe. In "Caring for the Environment," Rogers's human characters and humanoid puppets dramatize how to listen, understand, empathize, and apply animal wisdom, showing how easy it is to change our viewpoint and turn our attention to care and cooperation.

Conversion

Rogers had his own experience of conversion. In a story he liked to tell about a pivotal moment in his life, he explained how he changed his mind about a sermon he heard. After boning up on homiletics at Pittsburgh Theological Seminary, Rogers went to hear a well-regarded minister preach only to be disappointed in hearing a substitute deliver the most poorly crafted sermon, which broke all the rules he'd recently learned. As he was about to complain to a woman sitting beside him, she whispered, with tears in her eyes, "He said exactly what I needed to hear." Rogers often tells this story and relays his astonishment. In his lecture "More Than We Know," delivered for the Sesquicentennial of Saint Vincent at the Saint Vincent Archabbey Basilica, he recounts how he made sense of that experience: "I thought about that for a long time, and finally I realized that I had come in judgment and my *friend* had come in need. The Holy Spirit was able to translate the words of that feeble sermon to speak to the need of my friend [...] a real mysterious gift for her, but ultimately a profound gift for me as well. That experience changed my life. Ever since, I've been able to recognize that the space between someone who is offering the best he can and someone who is in need is Holy Ground."

Although he does not use the word conversion, Rogers repeatedly mentions this experience as life-changing and pivotal, an experience that allows him to decenter himself and instead turn toward what others need. And, this experience clearly informs *Mister Rogers' Neighborhood*. Rogers further explains: "Even the space between the television set and the receiver in need (and who isn't in *some* kind of need) is Holy Ground: whatever we offer in faith can be translated by the Holy Spirit to meet the need of someone who is willing and able to receive it." Rogers clearly believes that God acts between people to propel love and kindness.

Rogers dilates on the lessons from this experience throughout his talk. He sees such Holy Ground as the space where the "caring nature of God" moves though the words and deeds of caring people. For Rogers, human beings are conduits for God's love. He calls God "the source of all forgiveness and love" and asserts that "love is stronger than anything." It is this love that has operated between the lackluster minister and the parishioner and Rogers himself and his television neighbor, the child who is watching at home.

Mister Rogers' Neighborhood consistently depicts growing and learning, often depicting ordinary instances when Rogers or King Friday or another character changes his or her mind after learning something new. In "Caring for the Environment," Rogers expounds on changing the way families see their relationship to the Earth through their household trash, the faraway ocean and its fish, and their relationship to animals, particularly goats. The multifaceted learning and growing and changing Rogers advances for children coalesce with the more specific concept of "ecological conversion."

In *Laudato Sí: On Care for Our Common Home*, Pope Francis speaks of "ecological conversion" as a "change of heart" that helps us to recognize "our errors, sins, faults and failures, and leads to heartfelt repentance" and a "passionate concern for the protection of our world." This ecological conversion acts to remove believers from a "utilitarian mindset" that sees value only in how things—including animals and the environment—can be used. He argues that seeing humans as apart from and above everything precipitates an "unethical consumerism bereft of social or ecological awareness." To keep us from devouring the world around us, Francis implies that most of us need an ecological conversion.

For Francis, an ecological conversion offers a new horizon which generates "a number of attitudes which together foster a spirit of generous care, full of tenderness." Ecological conversion celebrates the "gratitude and gratuitousness" of God's gift; care becomes joyous. This expanded concern includes animals, drawing us to a "loving awareness that we are not disconnected from the rest of creatures, but joined in a splendid universal communion," a consciousness of "the bonds with which the Father has linked us to all beings," the knowledge that "each creature reflects something of God and has a message to convey to us," and a demand that they have a value that "human beings have no right to ignore." Francis even insists that "[e]very act of cruelty towards any creature is 'contrary to human dignity.'"

Rogers reflects this kind of view of the natural world and reverential care, in particular for animals, in his own life. Rogers experienced a kind of conversion around his vegetarianism, reporting that he gradually cut meat out of his diet as he reckoned with his beliefs around the value of animal life. Adopting vegetarian habits in the early 1970s, he believed that respecting animals meant not eating them. He helped finance the magazine *Vegetarian Times* and signed a statement from Beauty Without Cruelty USA to protest fur sales. Michael Long, in *Peaceful Neighbor: Discovering the Countercultural Mister Rogers*, writes that, "[f]ar from anthropocentric, Rogers's pacifist approach to life extended to the animal kingdom" in his vegetarian practice. Long exposes how Rogers's faith played a major role in his vegetarian lifestyle, citing Rogers's profile in *Vegetarian Times* that begins with a faith statement, clearly connecting refraining from eating meat and participating in animal slaughter with God's love for all creation. Long and biographer Maxwell King both consider Rogers's statement that he couldn't eat anything that had a mother to explore his empathy for animals.

This view means that Rogers believes that animals should be cared for and respected. He seems to subscribe to Thomas Aquinas's view that "each living creature manifests the goodness of God by living according to its own nature and way of flourishing." Thus, each creature has their own dignity that must be honored. One has only to think of Rogers's loving interaction with the gorilla Koko, his candid discussion with his television neighbors about his feelings when his dog died, and how he treats his pet fish, tenderly burying one who died in his Neighborhood backyard, to witness Rogers's connection, love, and respect for nonhuman animals. However, Rogers's main way of communicating his message of care for nonhuman creatures is through puppets.

Conversion through Puppets

Victoria Nelson, in *The Secret Life of Puppets*, explains that puppets tap into the once popular belief that no boundary "between mind and matter exists, and moreover that 'dead' inorganic matter and we as sentient, self-conscious beings share a mysterious and direct connection with a second reality that lies beyond the material realm." This is how Rogers uses puppets. Drawing on the connections between mind and matter, puppets connect humans and animals in ecosystems. Puppets turn us around to see these links between creatures and care.

As Mark I. West points out in "Fred Rogers and the Early Use of Puppetry on American Children's Television," along with Henson's artistic Muppets, Rogers's consistent and important work with therapeutic puppets secured puppets a special place on educational television at a moment when they were leaving commercial television. Rogers puppets not only help children voice their inner feelings and speculate about imaginative scenarios, joyful and worrisome, but they also cultivate empathy with others, particularly with animals. Rogers's sense of compassion extends to all of creation, and his puppets do not simply provide slapstick comic relief but are pivotal instruments in cultivating empathy and compassion, turning from self-understanding and love toward others and also toward becoming an agent for change in the world.

Furthermore, what Sidney I. Dobrin says in "'It's Not Easy Being Green': Jim Henson, the Muppets, and Ecological Literacy" of Henson's oeuvre holds true for Rogers as well. Because Henson's Muppets, much like Rogers's puppets and costumed actors, blur the boundaries between monsters (think Lady Elaine and possibly Purple Panda), animals (like Daniel and Corny), and humans (such as the royal family), Dobrin argues that "lessons of difference, acceptance, and otherness should be considered in terms of the nonhuman equally with the human." Rogers, like Dobrin asserts about Henson, develops "ecological literacy" through puppetry that focuses on "a conscious awareness and understanding of the relationships among people, other organisms, and the environments in which they live." Indeed, in Henson's and Rogers's children's television shows, puppetry is a tool to understand social justice, from racism and speciesism to environmentalism.

Goats, Old and New

Rogers displays his concern about the uniqueness of animals in his "Caring for the Environment" series with goats. In the series, the puppet goats from Northwood have arrived to solve the trash problem in the Neighborhood of Make-Believe, and, on Friday, Lady Aberlin tells Neighbor Aber that she was wondering if the goats might just eat the whole dump, revealing the pervasive cultural stereotype that goats eat everything. Neighbor Aber replies, "Oh, no, no goats don't eat garbage. In fact, goats are very picky, they can go through a whole lot of stuff and find just what they want."

Neighbor Aber's words echo a similar conversation in Rogers's television neighborhood. Earlier in the episode, before the solution has been revealed, a real goat makes an appearance in Mister Rogers's neighborhood. On his way to the school, Mr. McFeely brings a goat, William, to visit with Rogers. When Rogers says that he thought goats would eat anything, like cans and such, Mr. McFeely responds, "He [William the goat] doesn't eat just anything. That's not true. He likes nuts, and grains, and he likes vegetables ... they're very particular about what they eat." Like Rogers, William is a discriminating eater, a vegetarian, and the conversation reveals false and uninformed assumptions about goats and their behavior.

Because these misperceptions have been cleared up, the dignity of the goats shine through and everyone can truly listen to their wisdom and accept their help to solve the trash problem. The goats will use their talents to divide up trash into different piles so that much of it can be reused or recycled. They possess a wisdom hidden in their own language and their own community that helps

Mr. McFeely brings a goat, William, to visit with Mister Rogers (episode 1620). Courtesy of the Fred Rogers Company.

others. Their uniqueness—not the dismissive stereotypes we have of them—solve the problem, and Rogers's insistence on the dignity of creatures is reemphasized. Furthermore, Rogers implicitly suggests that the human species also consider their practices when he implies that mindless eating is not natural to goats just as mass consumption is not natural to human beings.

Rogers turns around our assumption that animals are mindless and helps people see the dignity of each creature. Rogers explores how both imagination and technology can help us access goats' knowledge. The Old Goat puppet cannot speak English but only bleats. The only one, besides New Goat, who understands Old Goat is Lady Aberlin, who is consistently an empathetic and close listener for all the puppets. Using her broad imagination and incisive empathy, she translates Old Goat's messages for her neighbors. New Goat, as well as most of the other puppets, communicates in English. Rogers's puppets, here, turn the tables on the discussion around the trash catastrophe. Rogers's Old Goat's bleating require neighbors to turn to Lady Aberlin and turn to New Goat. Conversation—which has the same root as conversion—turns

Neighbors anxiously await the fax from the Northwood goats, which will indicate that the goats will help them divide the trash to scavenge what can be reused and recycled (episode 1620). Courtesy of the Fred Rogers Company.

relationships around and helps us see animals' connection to us and recognize their wisdom.

Rogers further turns things around by having the goats request a fax machine to communicate with their goat coworkers back in Northwood. The community of goats work together to agree on a solution and dispatch a team of goats to sort the trash. Puppet Queen Sara Saturday provides the fax machine, which she uses for her Food for the World work, exclaiming, "Isn't it wonderful? I love that machine. It's so helpful." It is the goats, the animals, who know how to solve problems, draw in their fellow goats for help, and use technology as an aid in the process.

The goats' wisdom goes beyond their problem-solving skills, as they appear to recognize their kinship and interdependency with other animals and recognize their ecosystems as homes. In Friday's culminating episode, New Goat and Old Goat watch "The Universe Today" with their neighbors. During a program break, rather than a commercial, the Neighborhood of Make-Believe's television set plays beautiful ocean scenery. In a response to Old Goat's bleating,

Ecological Conversion

New Goat exclaims, "I thought so, too; glad you didn't throw it [the trash] in the ocean" (episode 1620). Courtsey of the Fred Rogers Company.

New Goat exclaims, "I thought so, too, glad you didn't throw it in the ocean," which implies that Old Goat is referencing the television water scenes and Lady Elaine's idea to throw garbage in the ocean. Television, another communication technology, allows neighbors to see each other, appreciate each other's homes, and, like the goats, recognize that every place deserves care. Here, television has the power to reveal the ocean's beauty and dignity, but the goats possess the wisdom necessary to save, preserve, and care for it. Or, perhaps, people who can imagine what goats might say access the wisdom of universal care.

Adopting Animals

The wise goats help us to see Rogers's understanding of animals, not as inferior but as beings like us. Rogers does not stop there, however. Through puppets, Rogers helps us to see animals as family. King Friday, the puppet patriarch, is uncle to Lady Aberlin, a live actor. She and puppet Prince Tuesday are cousins. Puppet X the

X the Owl's cousin, Mary Owl, visits in "Mister Rogers Talks about Families" week, which aired during Thanksgiving 1985 (episode 1552). Courtesy of the Fred Rogers Company.

Owl's cousin is Mary the Owl, an actor dressed up in a costume. However, Rogers uses adoption to more clearly cross species and connect people with loving affiliation.

The weeklong series "Mister Rogers Talks about Families" first aired in November 1985, during Thanksgiving. In this week, Mary the Owl, an actor in an owl costume, comes to visit X the Owl, a puppet, who is her cousin. Mary the Owl plans a cousin reunion, but the party causes problems for Bob Dog, an actor in a dog costume, who has no cousin. This drama is resolved when platypus-child puppet Ana offers to adopt Bob Dog. Everyone, then, is welcome at the cousin reunion. Rogers's make-believe makes a literal point: we are all cousins—humans, animals, and puppets.

Adoption is further discussed as humanoid puppets Betty Okonak Templeton and James Michael Jones adopt a baby, Carrie Dell. Furthermore, Rogers discusses the adoption of his own sister and shows a video of the real families of actors on *Mister Rogers'*

Ana the platypus offers to adopt Bob Dog (episode 1554). Courtesy of the Fred Rogers Company.

Neighborhood. He maintains that all families are real, and all are based in love. Rogers visits penguins' families at Sea World. He plants an orange seed and talks about how oranges grow into trees, and later shows a picture and a video of birds who have made a tree their home. He visits with Mrs. Shiono, who makes origami birds and a puppet for Mister Rogers. Birds, like puppet X the Owl, are lovable, and so are their homes, the trees that grow like children do. Rogers links animals, trees, paper, and puppets to access multiple avenues to celebrate interconnection in a universal family love.

Rogers pushes his viewers to expand their own view of family connections. He wants people not just to respect difference and see their connection to other creatures but to have them care about them as if they were family. Extended, odd, or adopted families are made of people we should care about, being sure to include those who feel or are left out. Through fantasy and puppets, Rogers wants us to see the dignity of animals and, while honoring their difference from us, value them as family.

The adoption of a baby by Betty Okonak Templeton and James Michael Jones. In Southwood, Dr. Bill is checking in on the baby as Lady Aberlin learns that the baby has been named Carrie Dell Okonak Templeton Jones, who is named for her Uncle Keith, pictured above, as well as her adoptive mother and father (episode 1553). Courtesy of the Fred Rogers Company.

Double Vision

Rogers is clear about what is pretend and what is real. As seen in the sharp distinction between his television neighborhood and the Neighborhood of Make-Believe, Rogers wants the child to understand that people work the puppets. In approximately one dozen episodes, Rogers shows children how he works the puppets, reminding them that they are tools for self-expression and imaginative play.

In a 1974 episode, Rogers shows children his puppets and how he speaks in their voices. Interestingly, he speaks as every puppet except for Prince Tuesday. Of course, this is also the one puppet he displays that he does not voice. Yet, the point still holds that, in simply holding up the one and only child humanoid-puppet but not animating it, Rogers wants children to see that they must speak for themselves. It is no wonder then that Rogers encourages children to become

Rogers shows children his puppets and how he speaks in their voices in this 1974 episode (episode 1384). Courtesy of the Fred Rogers Company.

puppeteers. In Friday's episode of "Caring for the Environment," Rogers demonstrates for children how to make their own puppets. The weeklong series has included different examples of children playing with reused and recycled materials, but Rogers culminates this motif by showing how balls and napkins become humanoid puppets, George and Charlie, who star in their own television program inside a repurposed box and ride in a shoebox trolley.

Puppets are split and yet united with the puppeteer, resulting in what Kenneth Gross calls "the doubleness of the puppet," a peculiarity that evokes a "double vision." This doubleness can help Rogers's viewers wonder about their connection to other creatures and things. Through their creation of puppets, children play with an entity that is both them and not them. When speaking through puppets, one can communicate with a version of the self that is both estranged, into the puppet body, and is still connected to the self, articulated by one's own voice.

Through this double vision, children become artists, creating and crafting identities and worlds, and, by doing so, children come to better understand themselves and the world. Rogers shows the child the benefits of talking with oneself and, imaginatively, simultaneously, talking with another. A child who might wonder if she is not so distant from what might be trash understands that it is within her power to help transform trash into toys and see the inherent value in the self, other, and everyday things. In becoming puppeteers, children may learn that no one is trash.

Rogers also seeks to empower children when he encourages them to make their own puppets in Friday's episode. Through making and playing with puppets, children have access to the power to recycle trash and rehearse themselves, making feelings manageable and toys valuable. This "double vision" invests the self and the puppet with care and concern, and children develop the power to see and enact a system of circulating love. In becoming puppeteers, children add to themselves. They learn to enter into caring relationships with other things. They can become like Rogers: someone who clearly cares for them and their world. These added powers transform children into something more than they were.

Cyborgs

When Rogers animates his animal or humanlike puppets, such as Daniel Tiger, X the Owl, Henrietta Pussycat, King Friday, Queen Sara, and Cornflake, he imagines the self and the other and stages conversations among puppets and live actors. This other is both family and animal. For example, animal Daniel Striped Tiger seems to represent a tender version of Rogers as a child, while King Friday XIII seems to represent a comic version of Rogers as an authority figure. The puppets in the Neighborhood of Make-Believe have their own personalities, histories, and relationships. The puppets talk with each other and the live actors. They take on a life of their own, even as Rogers is clear that talking puppets are make-believe. It is a puppeteer who talks.

As evidenced in the use of his own puppets, Rogers hopes that when children use puppets to explore their many feelings that they can manage these feelings and love themselves. As is discussed by Susan Linn, a puppeteer and psychologist who worked with Rogers, puppets within the Neighborhood of Make-Believe are accepted with whatever feelings and ideas they have. In writing about King Friday, Linn explains:

> His beleaguered family and subjects tolerate the king's self-involved authoritarianism, but they all persist in feeling and thinking exactly as they please. In spite of these difficult tendencies, the king is at no time reviled. He is even capable of overcoming his flaws enough to change his mind or listen to reason. [. . .] Like Lady Elaine, and all the residents of *Mister Rogers' Neighborhood*, King Friday is loved and accepted with all of his faults, just the way he is.

As a result, puppets make one powerful. Children can voice dissent or any reckless or vulnerable feeling through the other of the puppet. Puppets can more readily allow children to express their anxiety "[be]cause all the thoughts and feelings expressed through a puppet can be safely attributed to a creature other than ourselves, we bring forth our inner world more freely and less self-consciously." Children can voice uncomfortable and powerful feelings. Through puppets, Rogers asks children to speak out the many conflicting and amplified voices in their own minds.

Children can recognize the puppet's voice as both their own and not their own and the puppet's feelings as their own and not their own, or maybe not their only, feeling. Children, who play with puppets in the fashion Rogers models, can cope with their own formidable feelings and respect the feelings and differences of others. Children are not a family's puppet, lacking their own voices in the manner of a parent's pet, doll, or accessory. Rogers avoids the often-made conflation of pet and child that demeans both when he insists that neither are silent and encourages children to speak.

In helping us do emotional work, Rogers's puppets make people cyborgs. Cyborgs are those who have technology connected to their bodies which enhance human powers. The enhancement, however, is typically thought of in terms of fire power: with more strength, or speed, or weapons. Instead, Rogers's puppets make humans a cyborg because they enhance the emotional power of people. Although low-fi and low-tech, puppets enable us to see, understand, and accept our own emotions that are reflected through the puppets. Moreover, in seeing the emotional life of the puppet that is both separate from and connected to us, we can see animals and other parts of creation similarly.

Following Donna Haraway's "A Cyborg Manifesto," cyborgs offer a powerful vehicle to trouble the boundaries between human, animal, machine, and, more broadly, nonhuman entity. Out of this project, care and cooperation, through what Haraway calls a "coalition" become possible between entities. This coalition recognizes kinship that is based not on identity but on affinity, seeing in each other a likeness. Rogers has the same project in this weeklong series. His puppets represent humans, animals, and even the thing of the puppet itself as full of life, unique, valuable, and capable of performing the work of care. Through these, we come to see that fish and children feel, go to school, have homes, and are vulnerable. Though distinct, they are connected, and both need to be cared for.

Puppets extend our emotional life beyond the self to other animals, things, and parts of creation. The extension also helps us to understand ourselves. The love we have for ourselves increases as we love the creatures around us. The only difference would be that, instead of calling it a "coalition," as Haraway does, Rogers would call it a neighborhood, making a claim that our connections are more intimate and religious.

Ecological Conversion

Noticeably, there are no fish puppets present in the Neighborhood of Make-Believe. Neighbor Aber and Patrice mention fish, but we do not hear from them. While Rogers insists that it is not difficult to imagine how fish might feel, especially about pollution, he respects that they make no sound. Rogers never gives fish a voice, neither in his neighborhood nor in the Neighborhood of Make-Believe, a place where many puppet animals and animal-costumed humans speak.

In Rogers's multi-species world, fish are their own selves who are impenetrable and private, unknowable and yet valuable. Perhaps this strategy also suggests that human children might also be silent at times, but we must still imagine what care and protection they need. Analyzing human-animal communication in children's media, Zoe Jaques, in *Children's Literature and the Posthuman*, suggests that listening to silent animals undoes the "distinctly human limitation of requiring a creature to speak in order to conceive of it having a voice." The voices of children and animals go beyond words.

Rogers's perspective aligns with the logic of philosopher Timothy Morton who, in his book *Humankind: Solidarity with Nonhuman People*, asks us to rethink species. Through Rogers's use of puppets, the animal becomes a person, people express themselves, and the puppet itself becomes a person. The puppets allow us to think of a nonhuman person, be it animal or thing. This move allows us to think of the two meanings of "kind" in "humankind." Animals, humans, and puppets are all the same "kind" of thing, and this similarity makes an interspecies affinity. Being different but also of the same "kind" makes us compassionate toward each other, makes us "kind." It is a vision of the world, a way to organize our living together, or, as Morton puts it, a "political program" that should guide environmental activism. The recognized and respected differences in the midst of connectivity and similarity of kind engenders relationships of empathy and love.

In this five-episode series, the "political program" of caring for animals begins with and centers on water and fish. As discussed in chapter two, Monday's episode begins with Rogers showing children a fish greeting card, announcing the "Caring for the Environment" theme by reusing that card. Polluting the oceans is a direct consequence of the overflowing dumps in the Neighborhood of Make-Believe's apocalyptic drama, as explored in chapter one. Water is even part of Rogers's personal life: he was known to swim every morning at the Pittsburgh Athletic Association—an exercise he featured in episode 1493—which was a kind of rededication of himself every day, an immersion in holy water. Amy Hollingsworth, in *The Simple Faith of Mister Rogers*, writes about his swims as a sort of daily "baptism." Rogers's swims through these worlds, connecting his own life, the lives of animals, and the lives of children, to create a caring world and attitude of care for the environment.

Ultimately, in "Caring for the Environment," water captures Rogers's appeal to an ecological conversion. It harkens to a kind of baptism that signifies our changed view of the world. In snorkeling, in examining nature photography, and in caring for his own fish tank, Rogers centers his study on angelfish. Children are like fish, and the fact that Rogers chooses angelfish, not the sergeant-major or other schools of fish, hints toward this religious aspect of his message. The fish are holy, sacred, agents of God's creation.

In fact, he shows Lady Elaine Fairchilde and King Friday XIII undergoing conversions. Lady Elaine easily dismisses her idea to throw trash in the ocean when Lady Aberlin suggests the fish would not like it. Her conversion is quick. Likewise, King Friday XIII, who has largely delegated others to solve the neighborhood's garbage problem, easily accepts the new tactics the goats offer. These conversions seem ordinary, without any anguish that might come from changing one's mind. In fact, Rogers has built such generosity and open-mindedness into these characters. Shea Tuttle, in her biography of Fred Rogers, insists that King Friday XIII is consistently "the model of conversion." She understands King Friday "might exert undue influence, wield unearned power, or overrule wiser counsel, but there is good news: he is capable of seeing a greater truth and, when he does, he can—without shame or defensiveness—turn and go in a new direction." Rogers uses his puppets to celebrate conversion.

Through puppets, Rogers turns his viewers around to help them see the world in new ways, making space for our own conversions.

Children and adults learn that animals have wisdom and are like family, and puppets provide us with a double vision to see our interdependence and emotional power for empathy in these relationships. Rogers hopes that his audience comes to see their connections with the nonhuman and generate care for them. He helps children recognize their own fanciness, and find themselves in a new world, connected to everyone and everything via the holy ground between them. For Rogers, all people and animals are neighbors, and are not consigned down to the depths but are all buoyant and floating together in a watery neighborhood.

Chapter Four

Playthings and Creativity
Reduce, Reuse, Recycle, and Co-Create

In *The Mister Rogers' Parenting Resource Book*, Rogers said that the "very best kinds of playthings are open-ended," those that a child can make conform to his or her unique fantasies and feelings. These toys are taken up into the child's imagination. They are the foundation for emotional strength and social development. As child psychologist David Elkind puts it, play helps children explore whatever is on their mind. Rogers agrees, writing, "Sustained attention to things tends to foster deliberate thought. Readiness to develop the capacity for deliberate thought begins very early as children engage in their own kind of thinking—daydreaming, fantasizing, and making up all kinds of activities that we call play." Therefore, imaginative play might begin by attention to some object, some toy, by which children can channel their play, but it expands to help children "foster deliberate thought" and work toward understanding themselves, others, and their world.

Not all toys are like this, though. Rogers is wary of what he calls "single action" toys, like many mass-produced toys, because they impose a direction on play. These types of playthings often make children follow a certain "formula," one set by the manufacturer rather than the child. Because of this, they are transitory and particularly vulnerable to becoming trash. These toys are objects of temporary gratification and thrown away after the fun is gone. They commercialize childhood and turn children into consumers. This is where play and toys connect to Rogers's environmental imagination.

In many episodes of *Mister Rogers' Neighborhood*, and particularly in "Caring for the Environment," Rogers encourages children to create their own toys by reusing discarded household objects. Toys become ecological objects that open up worlds and develop meaningful relationships. They have histories, futures, and meanings. They connect children to other people. As philosopher Jane Bennett describes, toys promote "interactive fascination" that inspires "deep attachment" and "even an energetic love of the world." They are pleasurable, a joy for children and adults. Rogers's homemade toys propels caring for one's self and all human and nonhuman things in the world. He uses children's play with recycled toys to court good feelings and reveal what it means to be alive.

Playthings and Object Lessons

Rogers's program is filled up with the objects of everyday life, from presenting items to viewers after he puts on his sneakers to field trips that show how things are made. It is a way he teaches. To borrow the words of Sarah Anne Carter, Rogers has a "flexible form of pedagogy." Through objects, children are "led to internalize, understand, or even create broader narratives," and this approach "attempted to transform children's daily experiences into learning opportunities." Rogers uses objects to explore the moral dimension of our world, exposing the relationships between physical things and invisible feelings. He often finds in objects evidence of social relationships, contributions of human ingenuity, and celebrations of the natural world. In this week's themed episodes about garbage and recycling, Rogers concentrates on consumer goods and homemade toys.

In Monday's episode, "Caring for the Environment," Rogers had a candid conversation around recycling with Mr. McFeely, who shows Rogers how he uses scrap paper both for his Speedy Delivery Service and to create simple books for his grandchildren. Mr. McFeely explains what a dump is and how his "community service for the week" is to do something about the local dumps, which are filling up fast. He offers "recycling advice" about reusing and not buying anything one doesn't absolutely need or wasting things. As Mr. McFeely leaves, he shows Rogers his delivery bicycle and helmet. Rogers makes the connection between saving things and self-care: "That safety helmet is something that saves you. You're interested in saving all sorts of things." At this point, Rogers sees an old paper bag, discarded in his lawn, which he realizes he must save. Saving this potential trash is how Rogers associates ideas of toys and play with recycling.

Paper Bag and Children's Play

Rogers begins with the worn paper bag discarded in his lawn. First, Rogers uses the bag as a part of a game. Here he recommends play as the avenue to access connections between things and people. In his yard, he uses it as a basket to roll balls into a "bag-ball game," as he calls it. Playing with reused objects turns trash into toys, taking consumerism out of the mix. It makes children creators rather than consumers. When his friend Marilyn Barnett, a physical education teacher, stops by to do some exercises, she interrupts Rogers's game. In this three-minute segment, the pair performs bicycle-kicks, pushups, and stretch their backs by turning their bodies into balls. Marilyn acknowledges their transformation into human balls by comparing them to the balls Rogers was playing with: "I guess you were playing with balls, too, when I came," Marilyn says.

By combining the bag-ball game and the exercising into a single scene, Rogers suggests a number of ideas that children could think about. Caring for our bodies is important, an act of love that helps us grow straight and strong. All things are embodied, ourselves as well as paper bags and balls. Human beings can imagine what it is like to be a thing, in this case a ball, by using our bodies and minds. Both mental and physical exercise are play. A child's play at being a ball encourages reflecting on relationships with things, how our bodies and beings intersect.

Marilyn and Rogers turn their bodies into balls during their exercises (episode 1617). Courtesy of the Fred Rogers Company.

Rogers's "flexible form of pedagogy" continues when he suggests that the bag is alive. As Marilyn and Rogers play the bag-ball game, the bag itself animates and seems to want to play along. The bag leaps up as Marilyn's rolled ball jostles it. "Oh, you made it stand up!" Rogers exclaims. It looks as if the bag has sprung to life as one of Rogers's puppets. While it does not have a voice or a will, it still acts in the world. The way it acts in the world is not as a human being can, but it can bring surprises and joy by being a toy or part of play. Of course, if the bag is discarded as trash, it can act as trash does in the world with its slow decay, seepage, smells, and pollution.

The opportunities for learning that the bag offers continue on Tuesday when the bag returns to carry recycling materials. Mr. McFeely takes it to reuse with his other paper bags in his garage. Using the words of Stacy Alaimo, Rogers "entangles us in responsibility" to care for this paper bag that seems to be somehow alive. The paper bag is a natural material that may be reused and recycled. It is vulnerable and has a future. It can be part of our world as toy or helper. It could have been abandoned to litter our neighborhoods. Rogers and Mr. McFeely save it by reimagining it—which is also recycling.

Mr. McFeely takes Rogers's paper bag to reuse it (episode 1617). Courtesy of the Fred Rogers Company.

Paper Bag and Adults' Work

The lessons of the paper bag are far from over, and Tuesday's episode adds more messages for children and draws in adults about recycling. Rogers humorously implies that his play is not done in mentioning the absent balls from his bag-ball game: "Do you have any idea what I might have in this paper bag? Not balls, not an elephant, not a dining room table." In his silly list, Rogers prepares his viewers to understand that a little garbage can fill up a gigantic dump. He explains that he is ready to do some work. In his bag, he carries empty cans and glass bottles, which "people in our family have thrown them away because they don't need them anymore. But there's one more thing we can do with them. We can help them to get recycled. [...] If I take them to the recycling place then they won't have to fill up some dump somewhere." They need not be trash. In fact, his language suggests that the items do not want to be trash.

Rogers suggests that objects belong in our world, and it is our job to care for these things, like paper bags and used bottles. Children care for them when they reuse them for play and adults by recycling them. Rogers clearly invokes the obligations of his adult audience

Rogers steps on a scale at the recycling center (episode 1617). Courtesy of the Fred Rogers Company.

in this segment: "Did you find anybody who knows what recycling means? Well Mr. McFeely knows the location of the place where people actually take cans and bottles and start to recycle them." The "flexible form" of these lessons of the paper bag speaks to parents and children during this field trip to the recycling center. While Rogers insist that human beings are the ones who have more power to act in the world than the object, he tasks adults with greater responsibility, especially to use their power to recycle.

When they arrive at the recycling center, Mr. McFeely and Rogers weigh their cans, bottles, and cardboard. Rogers steps on the scale and opens up another learning opportunity. Like his gesture to turn into a ball in the previous episode, Rogers positions himself as a recyclable object. In a playful way, Rogers's viewers may wonder how people are recyclable. Because of Rogers's insistence that people are not trash, they are not discarded, but, like paper and glass, they can have different roles to play and different futures to explore. It is just a momentary opening for reflection, and it ends quickly with a smile and laugh from Rogers.

Rogers with safety glasses on examines crushed cans (episode 1617). Courtesy of the Fred Rogers Company.

Rogers's moment on the scale doesn't last long because Rogers is clear that children are not toys and people are not things. People are not manufactured. They (like animals) have feelings and should not be used the way things are used. The careful workers with their safety glasses and gloves may reassure children that human beings do not go into the recycling machines! And Rogers's paper bag, too, was saved by Mr. McFeely and does not join the paper items in the box crusher.

Insisting that people are not things is an important point for Rogers as he knows some children and adults alike might wonder if they are things, or mistakes, or accept mistreatment and misunderstanding. Rogers even raises this question for children when, in one of his famous episodes from 1987, Daniel Tiger wonders if he is a mistake, since he is tame and unlike any other tiger. Rogers reflected on that idea in that episode during a speech at a Public Broadcasting Service meeting: "I remember the day I wrote that script and that song thinking to myself how easy it is to fall into the trap of believing that just because we're not like everybody else there's something wrong with us—we're a mistake." Instead, Rogers insists that each person is always beautifully and importantly different from the next and that educational television, like *Mister Rogers' Neighborhood* needs to be a "life-enhancing gift [...] a gift of moral strength and respectful values" that explores the preeminent and originary value of each individual's inner self.

Rogers repeats this emphasis. In his 1998 "TV Critics Speech," Rogers passionately asserts that mass media producers and purveyors have a responsibility toward children to help them reject violence and cruelty and instead help children "become aware—at the deepest levels of their being—that they are lovable [...] because they're 'one-of-a-kind,' believing that no one they ever meet is an accident." Thus, for Rogers, respect for one's self and others is bound together. As is always the case, Rogers lifts people and things up, even potential trash, to the realm of human caring. When we play at objects becoming alive, at animating toys, and at being an object, we connect with these things and thus come to care about them. And people need to care—trash cannot take care of itself!

For his adult viewers, Rogers recommends recycling as an important way to care. He shows them what it would look like to collect materials and bring them to the recycling center. As with almost every moment in the episode, this knowledge is an opening to further learning. Rogers persistently uses factory field trips and videos of factory work to highlight that workers are caring when they help produce goods people use and enjoy. Tim Libretti, in "Dis-Alienating the Neighborhood: The Representation of Work and Community," explains how Rogers insists that relationships with objects indicate relationships with people. Realizing how people are connected to manufactured and homemade goods—from crayons made in a factory to Rogers's sweaters made by his mother—allows Rogers to propose "that we are engaged in broad and expansive sets of relationships in which people we don't even know are taking care of us and working to meet our needs, to provide for us. This behavior, rooted in the reality of our radical interdependence as a society, is a kind of love." Rogers consistently insists that things spring from human innovation, labor, and love.

At the recycling center Rogers goes even further in moving from a factory focused on production to an industry investing in reproduction, greening the assembly line and interrogating the long life of raw materials. As an analog to Rogers's touchstone factory trips, the trip to the recycling center positions the family, including children, as caring creators, not consumers, partnered with adult workers and recycling machines to care for things, each other, ourselves, and our world.

This view of our world is reflected in the trash catastrophe in Neighborhood of Make-Believe, detailed in chapter one. Here, Rogers employs the factory as a part of the solution to the garbage crisis. Cornflake S. Pecially, the factory owner, has been producing nose muffs to help neighborhood citizens deal with the garbage smell while giving an employee, an adult humanoid puppet named Hilda Dingleboarder, time off the assembly line to invent her own recycling machine. Again, it is paper, in the final episode of the week, that the machine transforms from trash into a paper fan, and, then again, into a paper crown. These renewed paper products become tools and accessories that signify how objects can empower people, in this case, to help them fan away the garbage stench they have created and convey the authority human beings have to mistreat or save things. Hilda Dingleboarder's invention and all solutions to the garbage crisis are coordinated and enacted by grown-ups: human, animal, and puppet adults.

Furthermore, Rogers's trip to the recycling center, which features families recycling, implies that this kind of care needs to be managed by adults. While children may save and sort recyclables, with adult help, Rogers proposes they care in their own sphere. He sings "I Like to Take Care of You" three times during this episode, first before and after feeding his fish. Between singing, Rogers asks: "Do you have anything that you take care of: a pet, or a toy, or a pillow, or a blanket, or a mom, or a dad? If you do, you can sing a song like that to them: I like to take care of you, yes I do, yes I do. I like to take care of you, yes I do, yes I do." Notice that Rogers does not mention trash, but he does mention toys. In singing the song twice, he suggests that children first need assurance that they will receive care and then they are able to give care to others.

Later in Tuesday's episode, after showing children how to make toy trees from reused toilet paper tubes, he sings the song again. This time, he more pointedly asserts that children care for the things of the world by reusing them to make their own toys. Rogers defines recycling as an expression of caring. He invites both children and adults to take particular caring actions and experience the good feelings that come with acting out of love. He asserts that adults must care for children and to do so they must safeguard their world. Recycling is both caring for the environment as well as caring for one's own children.

Blocks, Puzzles, and Playing Together

On Tuesday, in the Neighborhood of Make-Believe's emerging trash crisis, Corny throws out scraps of wood, which Lady Aberlin is determined to save. However, she is not sure what she will do with these miscellaneous pieces. Rogers provides the answer in his television neighborhood. He shows his viewer wood blocks that a caring adult friend has made from wood that was going to be thrown away. Rogers explains that children can play, building and rebuilding buildings.

Furthermore, Rogers explains the connection to the field trip: "The whole idea with blocks is you can build one building, and then you can use the same blocks to build another building. That's recycling right there! Use the same thing over to do something else. You can make all sorts of things. That, plus your imagination." Here, blocks expose that ecological play is endlessly regenerative and infinitely rehabilitative. Ecological toys are handmade, reused, support multiple avenues for play, and are interactive and often social. These

Cornflake S. Pecially throws out scraps of wood, which Lady Aberlin is determined to save (episode 1617). Courtesy of the Fred Rogers Company.

blocks, too, come alive; once a child creates a neighborhood out of blocks, that neighborhood can host any number of dramas.

Besides playing with recycled or reused materials that adults make into toys, children can even make their own toys from household goods, acting in a way consistent with Rogers's friend who made the blocks. Rogers complements the building blocks by adding homemade crafts. He uses toilet paper and paper towel tubes to make trees, setting them beside the blocks to green the setting. He explains that a teacher taught him to make these crafts when he was little. While giving concrete examples to adults and children, he goes beyond suggesting playthings. Rogers's admiration and gratitude for his teacher serve to position Rogers as a former child who is now a healthy and caring adult.

For Rogers, play itself connects children with adults, inspiring both adults and children to build a better world. In playing at building, children can imagine themselves growing up to be positive

Rogers builds with blocks made from discarded wood and discusses the connection between imagination and recycling (episode 1617). Courtesy of the Fred Rogers Company.

adults—working as engineers, architects, construction workers, artists, teachers, and parents—who care for the world and the things in it.

Rogers's "flexible form of pedagogy" continues on Wednesday when he brings a wood puzzle box to show his viewers. Rogers explains that, like the wood building blocks, someone made the puzzle out of wood that someone else was going to throw away, highlighting how individual people can make powerful and meaningful choices. He relishes the artistry, saying, "It's beautifully made, and I want you to see these different parts. Imagine making this!" He adds, "All the things that people can do! And to think someone might have thrown this wood away." Rogers delights in the many nested drawers that multiply the inside of the puzzle box.

In turning the puzzle inside out, Rogers reveals how surprising its interior spaces are and how many secret containers fill the spaces within the polished box. The inside is bigger than the outside. This puzzle is the flipside of the blocks from the previous episode. The wood blocks represent how our imaginations can rethink our use of

This wood puzzle is made of reclaimed wood and gestures toward children's inexhaustible inner life as Rogers finds hidden drawers (episode 1618). Courtesy of the Fred Rogers Company.

things, a kind of inside life turning around the outside world. While the blocks example is about the outside of things, the wooden puzzle reveals inside realities.

Not done yet, Rogers ends the sequence by showing his viewer that he cannot put the puzzle back together. He leaves it on the kitchen table and at the end of the program returns to find he still cannot solve the puzzle. He states, "This puzzle is too difficult for me to put back together by myself, so I'm going to ask a friend to help me to do it. Sure. It's a good feeling that you don't have to solve everything by yourself. You can always ask for help." Rather than a failure, Rogers's affect suggests that complicated puzzles, like caring for the environment, require people working together. Learning and problem-solving should be collaborations. Here, Rogers acknowledges the real and fortunate truth that we are never alone.

The puzzle's intricate, interlocking pieces also express another set of interlocking lessons for Rogers's viewers about the relationship between parts and the whole, individuals and society, children and their families. Here, the little pieces are greater than the whole. The wood puzzle's insides seem to grow and grow, becoming bigger than the shell that contains them, as Rogers takes out the little hidden drawers. The pieces look too big to fit inside the puzzle. While we know this is not true, we saw Rogers taking the pieces out, the optical illusion manifests the truth of the important insides and the large little things. Rogers, here, seems to anticipate Timothy Morton's ecological philosophy which maintains that the whole is less than the sum of its parts. He stresses that the part—me, you, the polar bear—is not replaceable. We are not mechanisms with replaceable parts, simple components in a system. He explains that "the whole and the parts are distinct in such a way that the whole doesn't totally swallow up and dissolve the parts, the parts matter a lot."

Rogers recognizes the inside parts of puzzles and people as valuable. He does so explicitly in transitioning from this moment with the puzzle to his closing song and its refrain that celebrates children "growing inside." The size and weight of our interiors is always bigger than our bodies and yet contained within our bodies. Rogers's toy puzzle is an incredible way to think about the relationship between parts and whole and between inside and outside. He dignifies each small action a child makes toward living in harmony with him or herself, neighbors, things, and ecosystems. Furthermore, he implies that the small child is as worthy as the adult, and that each family member has a place where they fit in.

Television and Global Work

Rogers most important toys appear in the final, Friday episode, culminating lessons about children's powerful play. Rogers shows children how to make simple puppets and turn a cardboard box into a television. Mr. McFeely arrives with a gift from Mrs. McFeely, a replica of Trolley that she has made from a shoebox. With this particular collection of homemade toys, Rogers prepares children

Reduce, Reuse, Recycle, and Co-Create

Rogers shows children how to make simple puppets and turn a cardboard box into a television (episode 1620). Courtesy of the Fred Rogers Company.

to recreate his television program. He shows children how to make these playthings in order to recycle the ideas and narratives on *Mister Rogers' Neighborhood*, making their own version of the program starring themselves.

Rogers was diligent and directive about what he wanted for his television program, and he had great control over every aspect of its production. He felt a calling and a power to reach children through television. In his book of collected wisdom, *You are Special*, Rogers talked about this relationship to feelings of control: "One of the greatest paradoxes about omnipotence is that we need to feel it early in life, and lose it early in life, in order to achieve a healthy, realistic, yet exciting, sense of potency later on." Rogers enabled children to be powerful during play, acknowledging that it's playing at being powerful. Rogers recognizes children's vulnerability and continually validates children's feelings of their own vulnerability and powerlessness and desire to feel loved, accepted, and cared for. When Rogers demonstrates for children how they can play at being like him by creating their own television program, he shows them a sense of their own powerful play not only to do what he does but go beyond it in their own unique and creative ways.

For Rogers, the lessons surrounding the homemade puppets, trolley, and television toys are multiple. As discussed in chapter three, children making and playing with their own puppets helps them access a dual identity to talk with themselves and imagine other human and nonhuman voices. Trolley helps children think about visiting different neighborhoods and imaginary places to expand their notion of interconnected neighbors. Likewise, the television, as a kind of toy, has the capacity to reveal our interdependence and connect people who may never meet—in this case, all of Rogers's mutual friends who are neighbors of neighbors. A real television is a cherished toy for both children and adults. Its programs can entertain and inform you or distract and deform you. The device comes electrically alive, projecting live people and moving pictures that create narratives and worlds to imagine the past and predict the future. It is this lesson which is primarily addressed in "Caring for the Environment."

In the Neighborhood of Make-Believe, Rogers models the best of what television can do while reminding children that television can be garbage. Mayor Maggie comes to watch Lady Elaine and King Friday on television in the Neighborhood of Make-Believe because her own television in Westwood is "full of garbage." While she means this literally as all the surrounding neighborhoods deal with their overflowing dumps, it is also a critique of television.

For a positive example, Rogers embeds another television program into the week, one tuned in to cosmic matters, a talk show called *The Universe Today*. As discussed in chapter one, Lady Elaine Fairchilde suggests that they seek outside counsel for their garbage crisis and she and King Friday take the purple jet to outer space to ask the entire universe for help. On this talk show, callers relay messages, concerns, and suggestions. Television is a way to work out problems and bring people far and close together.

The Universe Today connects people, puppets, animals, and things throughout the galaxy while localizing actions by finding the garbage solution in the very neighborhood from which it originated. When global and domestic relationships are in harmony, everyone is in tune. As mentioned in chapter two, King Friday's "Universal Gratitude" bass violin performance celebrates this attunement. When the weeklong disaster changes course and everyone works together to create a better world, the pleasures of pretend play are redoubled in the pleasures of care.

Playthings and Cocreation

Rogers insists that making one's own playthings is both work and play, and it performs the incredible function of nourishing both the self and the world. He repeatedly demonstrates how people can turn physical trash into meaningful play experiences. In turning a lost sock into a puppet or a used bag into a catching game, Rogers also turns materiality into feeling, turns an othered object into self-expression, turns a commodity into a gift, turns play into work, and even proposes to turn indifference—if not disgust—into love and care.

In his "Encouraging Creativity" commencement address given more than twenty years before the "Caring for the Environment" series, Rogers powerfully couples the individual person and the natural world to show that both are worthy of love and care. Rogers insists that we are "rare and valuable," that each person has "something which no one else has—or ever will have—something inside which is unique to all time." Rogers compares this specialness to the uniqueness of our Earth using the same vocabulary:

> You know it well may be that our planet, Earth, is the only spot in the entire Universe which can sustain human life. Of all the worlds we may be the only one where there has ever been—or ever will be people! That's sort of like someone saying to you that there is only

one square inch of soil on this Earth that can grow anything—and that square inch happens to be in your own back yard. You look at that soil of yours with infinitely greater appreciation when you become aware how rare and valuable it is.

Rogers maintains that each "rare and valuable" person has something to contribute, and this something is our own unique creative energy which can be used to marvel, wonder, and work toward creating "a sane design for living." His speech makes it clear that part of that design must be to work in harmony with our natural world.

Rogers further advances his ideas about the value of creative acts in a *New York Times* column called "Nurturing Creative Energy" in 1983. In this essay, Rogers admires "human creators" who work to bridge the gap between what the world is like and what we want it to be. Taking a firm stance, he proclaims, "Encouraging a child's (and one's own) enjoyment of, and participation in, human creative endeavors is, I have come to believe, the basis for every accomplishment that has made a difference in our lives, throughout history." Creative acts, for Rogers, are the most powerful agent of change in all time for all people.

For Rogers, these powerful creative acts are work and play and have the incredible potential to align with and reveal God's creative acts. William Guy, in "The Theology of *Mister Rogers' Neighborhood*," discusses Rogers's demand for a creative spirit in characterizing how Rogers asks his audience to work hard on all their endeavors. Guy stresses that Rogers demands his listeners honestly and actively strive to discover the truth about themselves and others, which Guy identifies as a radical theology. Guy explains: "Truth, in the theological outlook that Mister Rogers adumbrates, is not something imposed upon unwilling people 'from on high,' or something they are made to swallow unwillingly, 'in a spirit of obedience'; truth is something that they themselves help to define, that they contribute to." This is the same type of creative participation required for cocreation in an environmental spirituality.

Rogers hopes that people create a better world by using their creative energy in a way that celebrates God's creation. This kind of human creativity can be understood as cocreation, in that these creative acts collaborate with and extend God's creative endeavor. In Rogers's lectures, he occasionally mentions that "we're the part of creation God has identified with most." In asserting that "we are partners with God in forgiveness," Rogers suggests that we can be partners with God, do the work that God does, like God does, in creating a world in harmony with Creation. And it follows that human beings have a special responsibility to create, like God, and with God, a better world. In "Caring for the Environment," creating playthings, like creating artwork, takes care of the thing, nurtures the child's own imagination, and celebrates and extends God's creativity. Furthermore, this play is cast as environmental activism, helping children to make a difference in maintaining a clean and beautiful Earth. Such creative acts are acts of love, and for Rogers, they bring good feelings.

Good Feelings

Rogers's songs, which open and close every episode, taken together, work in harmony. The opening song of the neighbor celebrates community by proximity: "Since we're together we might as well say, would you be mine, could you be mine, won't you be my neighbor?" This song is an acknowledgment of our togetherness. The closing song about good feelings celebrates the recognition of growing and learning in dialogue, of the process of change in the self and in others that signifies aliveness. This song promises us all a real and lasting joy.

This point is clear in Rogers's weeklong program. At the end of Monday's episode, Rogers asks, "Do you know what recycle means? Well, if you want to, ask someone you know and next time we're together we can talk about it. Do you like to find out new things for yourself? I know I do. Discovering things about yourself and your world can give you a very good feeling. I'll be back next time. Bye." Rogers's questions and affirmations here open up to the play, recycling, work, and imagination, the "flexible form of pedagogy," for the whole week. It also opens up children to taking these ideas into their own homes and neighborhoods, an idea that Rogers believes will give them a good feeling.

Friday's episode bookends Monday's moment. While playing with the homemade puppets, trolley, and box TV, Rogers explains their connection to the "good feeling." He begins with his key word around creating and playing: "proud."

> You can use just anything for your play. In fact, when you make up things yourself, and have all kinds of play with the things that you just have around the house yourself, I'm really proud of you. "I'm proud of you, I'm proud of you. I hope that you're as proud as I am. I'm proud of you, I'm proud of you. I hope that you are proud of you, too."

Rogers then returns to playing with the toy studio and voices the puppets George and Charlie to say that they are proud of each other and decide to go in the trolley. Afterwards, Rogers continues speaking to his viewers: "When you feel proud about who you are growing to be, then you'll be able to feel proud about who your friends and neighbors are growing to be. That's a good feeling, when you can feel proud about somebody else." And he then sings his signature closing song:

> It's such a good feeling, to know you're alive. It's such a happy feeling, you're growing inside. And when you wake up, ready to say, I think I'll make a snappy new day. It's such a good feeling, a very good feeling, the feeling you know that I'll be back when the day is new, and I'll have new ideas for you, and you'll have things you'll want to talk about, I will, too.

And I imagine you do have a lot that you can talk about, and I hope that you'll talk about things that you can do to take care of yourself and other people and this wonderful world that we have. I'll be back next time!

Rogers beams with the contagious joy he feels. He expressed confidence in the child and adult viewers to advocate for themselves, for others, and for the natural world. He implies that playing, working, and cocreating—actions of caring for one's self, others, and the natural world—bring about such good feelings.

Chapter Five

"Tree Tree Tree"
The Joy in Rogers's Ecological Worldview

"Tree Tree Tree" is one of the most important songs in *Mister Rogers' Neighborhood*. It bookends Rogers's thirty-three-year series as he sings it in the very first and in the very last week. It is one of the most frequently sung songs in *Mister Rogers' Neighborhood*. It occurs more than twenty-five times. Its words are simple:

Tree tree tree
Tree tree tree
Tree tree tree
Tree tree tree
We love you
Yes we do
Yes we do
We love you
Tree tree tree
Tree tree tree
Tree tree tree
Tree tree tree

The song is even more common than it seems. As an instrumental composition, it is performed during interludes and soundtracks at various moments throughout the run of *Mister Rogers' Neighborhood*.

Rogers shows children how to make paper trees, and, briefly, the signature melody of "Tree Tree Tree" cascades from the piano (episode 1620). Courtesy of the Fred Rogers Company.

"Tree Tree Tree" is so common throughout *Neighborhood*, and its melody so infectious, that it resonates even without its lyrics.

"Caring for the Environment" includes one such instrumental version of the "Tree Tree Tree" melody. In the second episode, after visiting a recycling center, Rogers shows children how to make paper trees, and, briefly, the signature melody of "Tree Tree Tree" cascades from the piano. Rogers comments that paper is "easily recycled!" and explains how making toys for yourself is a way to take care of yourself. He implies that reused domestic objects turned into homemade toys creates a network of care, for the other, the world and its trees, and the self. Rogers sings "I Like to Take Care of You" and tells children that they can sing that song to themselves.

The song is a clue to Rogers's view of the world. Its love of trees and its echoes in the "Caring for the Environment" week indicate the importance Rogers places on the environment. More than this though, its recurrence reveals that Rogers's environmental concern is not an issue off by itself, celebrated for a week and forgotten. Importantly, Rogers's environmentalism is part of a much larger view of the world, a world where we are to care about all things.

It is a perspective that Rogers built throughout the course of his program, an uplifting message of a love that extends toward all, including creation itself. "Tree Tree Tree" expresses the deep roots and expansive branches of Rogers's ecological imagination.

Lullaby: Love in the Home

Even before the first national broadcast of *Mister Rogers' Neighborhood*, on February 19, 1968, Rogers sang "Tree Tree Tree." The *Neighborhood*'s precursor, *Misterogers*, debuted in 1962 on CBC Television (the Canadian Broadcast Company). In 1966, Rogers moved the program to Pittsburgh, creating *Misterogers' Neighborhood*, later called *Mister Rogers' Neighborhood*. It was picked up for regional broadcast by the Eastern Educational Network, a forerunner of today's American Public Television. Thus, from 1966 to 1967, *Neighborhood* was available beyond the Pittsburgh area, also running in Boston, Washington, DC, Chicago, New York, Miami, and San Francisco. In the 100 programs made with EEN, Rogers sang "Tree Tree Tree" at least five times, according to Emily Uhrin, archivist at the Fred Rogers Center.

The song has deep roots for Rogers. It is connected to his own childhood, as he explains in a latter 1971 episode. His younger sister liked to hear him sing "Tree Tree Tree." It is easy to imagine him at eleven years old, singing it to his baby sister. In the early episodes of *Mister Rogers' Neighborhood*, "Tree Tree Tree" functions most consistently as a lullaby, including in episodes 0002, 0030, 0040, 0045, 0060, and 0113, among others. The six-word song is propelled by a simple, soothing melody and suggests a love that is beyond words, or that does not need words; it is an understanding and confidence in love. As a lullaby, "Tree Tree Tree" connects peaceful slumber and safety with family love, neighborly love, and love for nature as our common home. It prepares children to meet the world with gratefulness and joy.

This point is made clear in episode 0002 from 1968. In this first nationally broadcast week, Lady Elaine has used her magic boomerang to move structures around in the Neighborhood of Make-Believe. In this same episode, Rogers talks about how change can provide an opportunity for learning and growth. However, in the Neighborhood of Make-Believe, King Friday establishes border guards and plans for war against the changers. Lady Aberlin confronts King Friday and his war-making with a song to praise the afternoon: "It's Afternoon, Let's Sing About It!" This song prepares us for the praise and joy in Rogers's "Tree Tree Tree."

Rogers reinforces this connection. In his television neighborhood, he talks about the afternoon song and then sings "Tree Tree Tree" as an evening, bedtime song. He sits down and calmly sings the song, looking straight into the camera. Both songs are affirmations of the natural world and both celebrations of love. And, here, they are rooted in the comfort and stability Rogers's offers in the face of episodes about change. In fact, a similar change-oriented scenario happens again a few months later. Also, in 1968, in episode 0030, Lady Elaine turns things upside down in the Neighborhood of Make-Believe. Like her previous rearranging, this discomfort and unease is assuaged, in part, when Rogers sings "Tree Tree Tree" at the end of the program. The song, it seems, is meant to console and comfort children, making them less fearful of the changing world around them and more prepared to encounter change with ease, welcome, and even joy.

On multiple occasions, Rogers uses "Tree Tree Tree" as a comforting lullaby for families securely in their homes and even extends its meaning further to include nature as a common home. Returning to episode 0002, when Lady Elaine first rearranges the neighborhood, Rogers remarks that the song reminds him of the tree that is the home of X the Owl. Rogers prompts viewers to consider how they should understand home, and he suggests that they should do so in ways that differ from King Friday who attempts to barricade his home against people, afraid to welcome strangers. The comforting

Rogers sings "Tree Tree Tree," looking straight into the camera in an early episode from 1968 (episode 0002). Courtesy of the Fred Rogers Company.

lullaby of "Tree Tree Tree" inspires gratitude and joy, rooted in comfort and stability. A home is a place of safety for the family that lives there, as well as others who are welcome to visit. Rogers expands joy by helping people see others' joy in their homes.

Rogers continues to emphasize that a home is secured not by being withdrawn into itself and isolated but rather by being connected to other homes and other people. In episode 0045, from 1968, Rogers presents a short opera about a mother leaving and coming back. The grandfather sings the song "Tree Tree Tree" as he rocks his grandchild to sleep. In the opera, the mother comes back, of course, while her child is sleeping. While Rogers makes the point that loved ones come back, and babysitters can care for us, he uses "Tree Tree Tree" to celebrate the safety children can feel in their own homes as well as a home that is open to others.

These others not only sustain the comfort and stability of the home but also enrich the lives of the people within it. This is one of the many reasons why Yo-Yo Ma's famous visit in 1985 concludes with him playing, with Joe Negri, "Tree Tree Tree." Through his incredible cello playing, Ma can render both works by Bach and the simple "Tree Tree Tree" exquisite, showing how friends can enrich one's own life. Rogers's use of the song, then, suggests safety and comfort in the home, not by having it closed off, but precisely because it is connected to others, even others that might seem different from us.

For Rogers, neighborly connectivity extends across cultures. Focusing on children and mothers, Rogers pivots "Tree Tree Tree" to explore the common love mothers and children have for each other in multiple cultures. He does this by welcoming different languages and expressions of the song. In 1971, Queen Sara Saturday sings "Tree Tree Tree" to a visiting Finnish singer, Barbara Koski. Queen Sara explains that she sings it as a lullaby when she's babysitting. Ms. Koski proceeds to sing "Tree Tree Tree" in Finnish. With so few words and a simple message of love, "Tree Tree Tree" is a perfect choice to cross languages, cultures, and traditions.

Likewise, in the 1993 week on the subject of "Love," Rogers's visiting musician, Ukrainian American Peter Ostroushko, played his mandolin and sang, in Ukrainian, one of his mother's favorite songs. Then, accompanied by Joe Negri, he celebrates good feelings by playing "Tree Tree Tree." Ostroushko's pairing of the two songs celebrates his love for his mother and love for trees. This happens again! In 1996, Rogers visits Negri's Music Shop, where Jabali Afrika is rehearsing. The musicians demonstrate their instruments, and the group plays their song "Appreciation to the Mothers" and "Tree Tree Tree." Here the love of the mother and the love of Mother Earth are in harmony. "Tree Tree Tree" is Rogers's go-to song for cross-cultural celebrations. It is so fruitful for translation and adaptation.

In 2001, in the last week of *Mister Rogers' Neighborhood*, Rogers uses "Tree Tree Tree" as a lullaby for the last time. After playing a few songs on his glass harmonica, visiting musician Dean Shostak, with Joe Negri on guitar and Rogers humming and singing along, perform "Tree Tree Tree." Understanding the song as a lullaby, Shostak explains that his six-month-old daughter loves the song. The three

Ukranian American Peter Ostroushko and Joe Negri play "Tree Tree Tree" on a 1993 episode (episode 1664). Courtesy of the Fred Rogers Company.

musicians then play it slowly and serenely. Shostak relays the history of his instrument, which was invented by Benjamin Franklin, and its celestial sounds inspired Mozart and others to compose for it. These details seem to suggest that the American statesman and inventor's creativity inspires collaboration and welcomes others' voices. Like many instances of "Tree Tree Tree," and in contrast to most songs performed solo in *Mister Rogers' Neighborhood*, it is a song that is sung with company. "Tree Tree Tree" establishes the importance of community, defining a neighborhood broadly by welcoming the natural world and all of creation into neighborly fellowship.

In all of these examples, Rogers grounds the song in comfort and security, as a lullaby that can quiet children's anxieties and soothe their fears. As a result, Rogers prepares children to hear in his song revelations about our place in the world. Within the context of his program, "Tree Tree Tree" exposes our common love of family, connects people in a global community, and translates the silence of the natural world into a song of love and adoration for Mother Earth. Rogers uses a children's lullaby as a celebration of our common humanity and our common connections, crossing cultural, ethnic, and geographic boundaries to figure "Tree Tree Tree" as global music. "Tree Tree Tree" acts as a universal song of our humanity, celebrated through a commonality with trees. It is natural to be connected to nature, and natural to be connected to each other.

Praise Hymn: Joy in the World

Not only is "Tree Tree Tree" the only song, other than the opening song, to be used in the first and last weeks of *Mister Rogers' Neighborhood*, it is also a high-frequency song during the entire run of the show. Along with the opening and closing song, and excluding songs that introduce characters, such as "Speedy Delivery," "Tree Tree Tree" is one of a dozen songs that occurs more than twenty-five times in the lifespan of the television program. Even though "Tree Tree Tree" is particular and unlike any of the others, it helps construct Rogers's worldview just as much as the other often-sung songs.

Tim Lybarger has accounted for each instance a song is sung in his indispensable online library, "The Neighborhood Archive." This work has revealed that "Tree Tree Tree" is joined by other high-frequency songs that nurture children's sense of self, help them explore their emotions, and encourage them to act in positive and productive ways. "I Like to Be Told," which occurs twenty-seven times, helps children recognize why they have anxiety and encourages parents to explain anticipated experiences to their children. "I'm Taking Care of You" is heard forty-seven times and reinforces the security Rogers hopes all children have from a beloved adult. "Please Don't Think It's Funny" and "What Do You Do (With the Mad That You Feel)?" occur more than thirty times, and both help children recognize and constructively deal with difficult and uncomfortable emotions. These songs help children find ways to become comfortable with themselves as they articulate their vulnerabilities, needs, and feelings. They assure children of their security.

Rogers includes a set of songs around accepting and loving each child, just the way they are. These songs about unique and special children occur most often. "Everybody's Fancy" praises the uniqueness of each individual's insides and outsides. While it occurs almost sixty times, its lessons are reinforced by "It's You I Like," which occurs seventy times, and "You are Special," which occurs almost ninety times! These songs explain how Rogers likes and accepts each child for who they are, not the things they have, and assert that they are a very special "friend" to him. These two songs work in harmony with "Many Ways to Say I Love You," which is sung almost fifty times. These songs, in part because of the first-person address, feel personal. The tone of each is buoyant. Rogers often encourages children to sing these songs to others. Rogers builds and maintains a world where acceptance and love are the defining attributes, supporting each individual and cultivating neighborliness.

Finally, Rogers has a set of songs that affirm children's success. "You're Growing," which asserts and celebrates the "fun" of growing up, works in concert with two other high-frequency songs that spur children to act. All three in this set occur around thirty times. "You've Got To Do It" emphasizes learning as part of growing up and tells children that their imaginative work is not done until they act on it. Finally, "I'm Proud of You" affirms the choices the child makes now, as well as in the future, projecting and celebrating good decisions and loving actions.

"Tree Tree Tree" is part of this collection of songs that maps out a world of caring, a world that begins with children feeling secure, accepted and loved, and in relationships and neighborhoods meaningfully connected to others. Yet, "Tree Tree Tree" is startling in its difference. Sung twenty-seven times and repeated voluminously in instrumental versions, the song grounds and energizes *Mister Rogers' Neighborhood*. There are only six words—"Tree [. . .] / We love you / Yes we do"! This song, in contrast to the others, is not about us, or other people. It is not about understanding and accepting anyone's feelings. It is not about our growing. There is no narrative, no apparent lesson. Rather, this song is about trees, about nature. And, it is about loving those trees, which are incontrovertibly different than us, stubbornly not like us. It is a song about celebrating that love.

Rogers seems to have had a special relationship to hymns of praise. In Amy Hollingsworth's *The Simple Faith of Mister Rogers*, she talks about Rogers's spiritual routines with a joyful morning hymn he'd sing before his daily swim. She writes, "Before diving into the pool, he would sing (out loud but not too loud) 'Jubilate Deo,' a song Henri Nouwen had taught him from the Taizé community in France. '*Jubilate Deo, Jubilate Deo, alleluia* (Rejoice in the Lord, rejoice in the Lord, alleluia),' he would sing and dive in. He emerged from the pool ready to face a new day with a fresh slate, as if wet from baptism." Clearly, this hymn is energizing. It is related to Psalm 100 in the Hebrew Bible of the Book of Psalms, translated as: "Make a joyful noise unto the Lord, all ye lands." And in the Latin Vulgate, it is Psalm 99 and begins, "Jubliate Deo" or "Jubilate" (closer to how Rogers sings the hymn).

Not only did Rogers offer a joyful praise song each morning, but he also seems to have used them to celebrate the wonders of the natural world. In a letter to Amy Hollingsworth, Rogers gives two options for celebrating a beautiful sunset he encounters from his retreat at the Crooked House in Nantucket: the doxology or silence. He writes to her, "In fact the sun is making its way to the sea as I wrote to you. Wish you, Jeff, Johnathan and Emily were right beside us this very instant. We'd probably all burst forth with the *Doxology*, either that or simply stand in silent wonder." Among Christian traditions a doxology is typically an expression of praise for God and creation. Widespread in Protestant traditions, the doxology, or the common doxology, is often rendered as this short prayer: "Praise God, from whom all blessings flow; / Praise Him, all creatures here below; / Praise Him above, ye heavenly host; / Praise Father, Son, and Holy Ghost. Amen." In many traditions, it is common in high hymns for the final stanza to take the form of a doxology. Doxologies occur in the Eucharistic prayers, the Liturgy of the Hours, hymns, and various Catholic devotions, such as novenas and the rosary.

While Rogers rarely used religious language in his program, as he was concerned about excluding children, his "Tree Tree Tree" can still be considered a hymn for children. Again, the words are simple and celebrate singing out our love for nature:

> Tree tree tree
> Tree tree tree
> Tree tree tree
> Tree tree tree
> We love you
> Yes we do
> Yes we do
> We love you
> Tree tree tree
> Tree tree tree
> Tree tree tree
> Tree tree tree

To joyfully affirm that we love trees stretches the imagination and energizes the spirit. Plants hardly seem to move, their leaves are basically monochromatic, their flowering and fruiting can hardly be called emoting, their motivation appears to be mindless inertia, and they are more or less silent. Often regarded as the lowest life form, plants and trees appear to "belong to a world of blind biological processes unfolding without order or purpose or meaning." Difficult to relate with, it's common for people to become inattentive to plants and uninterested in plant conservation. This tendency to ignore plants is so widespread that Elisabeth Schussler and James Wandersee, a pair of US botanists and biology educators, coined a term for it in 1998: "plant blindness." They described it as "the inability to see or notice the plants in one's own environment." Not only does plant blindness have consequences for our ecosystems, medicines, and mental health, but it estranges us from our home in creation.

By singing "Tree Tree Tree" as a hymn of praise, Rogers's simple song comprises some of the best strategies to reduce tree blindness. Schussler recommends "everyday interactions" with plants, as well as emphasizing plants in art and stories. The song quietly and insistently reminds families of the importance and beauty of trees. Its recurrence draws attention to plants not only in his week on "Caring for the Environment" but throughout the long life of *Mister Rogers' Neighborhood*. Furthermore, Rogers participates in alleviating plant blindness by helping people connect with plants in singing of our love for trees. Environmental psychologist Kathryn Williams of the University of Melbourne argues that those emotional connections are crucial for plant conservation. Williams expresses optimism about increasing empathy for plants. "It's not at all implausible," she says. "It's about imagination." And this is where Rogers excels. Rogers dignifies plants as he celebrates trees. Everything in the world is sacred to Rogers. He encourages us to sing out love and praise for living trees.

Finally, Rogers helps reduce plant blindness by proposing that we recognize trees as we recognize ourselves, as unique individuals who are growing, who need care, and are capable of giving it as well. In episode 1030, from 1969, Rogers's "Tree Tree Tree" forms connections between people and trees as Rogers juxtaposes his own uniqueness with the viewers and with trees. Tim Lybarger, in "The Neighborhood Archives," recalls that the program ends when "back at the house, Mister Rogers waves to viewers in his mirror and talks about his reflection. He reminds viewers that there is only one person in the world just like them. Suggesting that the same is true for all living things, he concludes by singing 'Tree Tree Tree.'" While people can act as if they are separate from each other and the world, the truth that Rogers sings is that we are connected, dependent on each other, indivisible from our neighborhood, and connected to creation.

Unsung Ballad: Dancing to an Ecological Love Song

When Rogers uses "Tree Tree Tree" to deal directly with the natural world, he grounds and advances an ecological imagination. In particular, Rogers uses "Tree Tree Tree" to highlight reusing and recycling. In fact, Rogers plays with the different types of repurposed, reused, and recycled instruments to produce "Tree Tree Tree." Just as all different people can sing the praise of the tree, this alternative instrumentation reveals all the things of the world, even things we might think of as trash, harmonizing joyfully.

In 1971, in a scene in Negri's Music Shop, Bob Trow and Johnny Costa are performing with guest Don Riggs by using only recycled items. They play "Everybody's Fancy" using old pipes and a screwdriver and an empty can and box before Mr. Riggs plays "Tree Tree Tree" using a hand saw. Together as a group, everyone plays "It's Such a Good Feeling" before Mister Rogers returns to the house and concludes for the day." These songs work together to expose an ecological imagination. "Everybody's Fancy" shows respect for the material body of each person, and each recycled instrument, complementing how the song comes to show the importance of animals discussed in chapter three. Already, though, in 1971, "Tree Tree Tree" celebrates the natural world, worthy of preserving, which recycling helps make possible. And "It's Such a Good Feeling" works to recognize the emotional benefits we get when we take care of things and the world, which is a way to take care of each other and ourselves. In this episode, the four men are laughing, rejoicing. They dance, moving around to play their instruments.

Rogers connects this exuberant moment with others like it to celebrate reuse. Back at the house in this 1971 episode, Rogers explains, "So many things to make music with; remember the time we had those glasses with water in them?" Rogers explicitly connects Don Riggs's work reusing things found in a junkyard to his own practice of reusing bottles, something much easier for children to do. Like

In Negri's Music Shop, Bob Trow and Johnny Costa are preforming with guest Don Riggs by using only recycled items in a 1971 episode (episode 1152). Courtesy of the Fred Rogers Company.

the recycling of memories in "Caring for the Environment," here he also reminds children to remember, a recycling of moments and ideas that access and hold foundational values, such as the ecological value to care for all things.

There are at least three instances when Rogers demonstrates how to fill reused bottles with water and turn them into instruments, including episodes 0034, 1364, and 1509. He chooses, each time, to play "Tree Tree Tree," which connects them to the ecological act of reuse. Creating one's own toy bottle organ is a playful act that Rogers celebrates. Easily recognizable as an instrumental piece, "Tree Tree Tree" also taps into reusing as a tactic to show care for things, nature, each other, and ourselves.

In his week on "Friends" in 1982, Rogers has borrowed the bottles from a friend and fills them with colored water to play "Tree Tree Tree," and, toward the end of the episode, "Many Ways to Say I Love You." Rogers lets us put the pieces together to represent that sharing with a friend, playing a song that celebrates trees, is all about love. He challenges children to see reusing objects to make their own

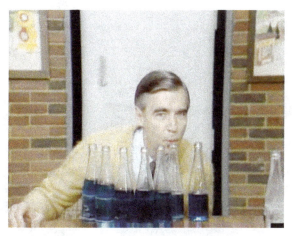

Rogers plays "Tree Tree Tree" with bottles in a 1982 episode on a week on "Friends" (episode 1509). Courtesy of the Fred Rogers Company.

toys and direct their own play as love, an imperative that is clear in "Caring for the Environment," particularly when the song is played while Rogers makes crafts in Tuesday's episode.

In the 1974 instance when Rogers reuses bottles to play "Tree Tree Tree," he connects that play to learning about trees in and of themselves. In the Neighborhood of Make-Believe we learn more about trees, as Lady Elaine tries to tap an oak tree in episode 1364 from 1974. Tim Lybarger reports that, in this episode, "In the Neighborhood of Make-Believe, Lady Elaine has set up a series of pipes to draw syrup from X's tree to her Museum-Go-Round. Handyman Negri and X remind Lady Elaine that his tree is an oak tree which produces no syrup. Chef Brockett and King Friday help Lady Elaine to remember that she used to use brown sugar syrup when she was a child." In his television neighborhood, Rogers's dark liquid in his bottles might be a brown sugar syrup. After this play, Rogers's recital of "Tree Tree Tree" from his bottles seems to acknowledge the fruit and syrup from trees as part of celebrating love for them. Perhaps, here, reusing the bottles becomes more closely connected with taking care of the natural

Rogers plays "Tree Tree Tree" with bottles in a 1969 (episode 0034). He reuses these bottles in 1974 in a similar scene. Courtesy of the Fred Rogers Company.

world and celebrating how it takes care of us, offering delightful fruits and sweet maple syrup.

This celebration continues in the earliest instance with a homemade bottle organ. In 1968, in episode 0034, Tim Lybarger, in "The Neighborhood Archives," describes how Mister Rogers arrives with an empty bottle that he has borrowed from a neighbor. He takes it to the kitchen, where he has several other bottles on the table, which appear to be the bottles he reuses six years later in the 1974 scene. With each bottle filled with different amounts of fruit juice, Mister Rogers uses them to play "Tree Tree Tree" and "Joy to the World." Moving to the other room, he plays the same songs on the piano. Rogers uses "Tree Tree Tree" in the context of his other songs to draw out what is being praised. Here, the easily recognizable "Joy to the World" places "Tree Tree Tree" in a religious context, most closely associating it with a Christian celebration of God's creation. To recite the song is to celebrate the Earth, both heaven and nature erupting in glory and praise.

In all these above instances, "Tree Tree Tree" is not sung, but the instrumental versions nonetheless resonate. Perhaps in the very absence of its words, children might find room in these performances to sing out themselves. The song is contagious. These are joyful renditions. The homemade instruments involve the whole body in a kind of celebration of trees and reuse that enlivens the performer and praises the beautiful natural world that is our common home.

Anthem: Trust in the Future

Rogers uses the song three times in his very last week, 2001's "Celebrating the Arts," twice on Monday and once on Thursday. It is the only repeated song, outside of the opening and closing numbers and Mr. McFeely's "Speedy Delivery." In the final week, "Tree Tree Tree" was clearly on Rogers's mind. While the song might at first seem to be about how nature can inspire art for this "Celebrating the Arts" week, it is really about an ecological worldview that has spanned the life of the program.

To introduce the week's theme, Rogers arrives with a small potted oak tree. The lessons of this actual tree are manifold. Mr. McFeely brings a second plant, a pine tree. Rogers suggests that each tree is different and unique, and, showing us the acorn and the pinecone, he implies that we are different from the very beginning. He makes the comparison clearer by comparing the plant and the child. He says he is "tree-sitting," which makes a clear link to babysitting, and he remarks, explicitly, "This tree grows just the way you grow," and sings "You're Growing." He proceeds to draw a picture of the tree and, although he does not feel he is a good artist in this way, his artwork is an act of love—a celebration of the tree and a gift for Mr. McFeely.

Rogers then assembles his real, potted trees with the Neighborhood of Make-Believe models on his kitchen table, highlighting how the real trees become part of the set. Transitioning to the Neighborhood of Make-Believe, the emphasis on trees continues. In contrast to X the Owl's Cousin Mary Owl, who lives in a sycamore tree, Henrietta remarks that she and X live in a "make-believe tree." An excited X, Henrietta, and Mayor Maggie sing and sign the first verse of "Tree Tree Tree" as they wait for Cousin Mary Owl's visit. Not a lullaby, "Tree Tree Tree" feels like an anthem sung in an energetic tone with an upbeat tempo. Mayor Maggie's signing is accompanied by Henrietta simply singing "meow meow meow," perhaps translating "Tree Tree Tree" into her own meow-meow language.

"Tree Tree Tree" is a rousing anthem for love. The song acts as a cheerful celebration for extended family as well as the trees itself, which the birds, and, in this case, a shy pussycat, call home. Cousin Mary Owl arrives and shares her videography, insisting that making videos is art. (Of course, Rogers, here, asserts for his adult viewer that children's television, too, can be and should be art, as discussed in chapter four.) Furthermore, Mary Owl's videos are all of trees, and the last shot is of the front door of the Owl Correspondence School, located inside a beautiful tree. The video makes Mayor Maggie want to dance and X the Owl want to sing. He and Cousin Mary Owl proceed to sing the "Owl Correspondence School" song, hinting that growing involves learning, practice, and concentration. Rogers uses trees to celebrate the natural world, to acknowledge trees as the homes and schools for animals, and to suggest growing up.

Finally, at the end of the episode, Rogers talks about his personal love for trees, remembering a favorite tree from his childhood. He explains, "I would talk to the tree and tell it how beautiful it was and how glad I was to live beside it. I guess I've always loved trees, ever since I was a little boy." He then sings "Tree Tree Tree" as he cleans up. When he walks over to the fish tank and feeds the fish, he modulates the song, singing "fish fish fish." The song, although originally about a love for trees which are our neighbors and help define our home, becomes a song to praise all of creation. In his final chat, he reveres the wonderful oak and pine tree seeds in his pocket, reminding us that they can grow into trees, which are "expressions of beauty, mmhmm, just like you." Rogers links trees with children.

Rogers suggests modifying the words to celebrate the animals and things you love in an episode from the year before as well, this time more explicitly. In 2000, in the Friday episode of the week on "Curiosity," Rogers visits Joe Negri's music shop and visits with teenage violinist Hilary Hahn. After she demonstrates her instrument and discusses playing as a young child, she and Negri play "Tree Tree Tree." Back at his television house, Rogers, after talking about the visit with Hahn, feeds his fish and sings, changing "Tree Tree Tree" for his fish: "Fish, fish, fish." We love you. Fish, fish, fish." He proceeds to explain, "I was just thinking, you could use any word you want for that song. Words of something you like. Like, pillow, pillow, pillow. Pillow, pillow, pillow. Or book, book, book. Book, book, book," as he takes the soft book he read earlier out of the "soft carrier" pillow. Rogers explains that curiosity helps us to think and feel about things, which drives our learning and growing. Curiosity leads to wonder, awe, and praise.

Sung as an exuberant anthem for love, "Tree Tree Tree" proposes that praise leads to action. When it was sung like a lullaby, "Tree Tree Tree" emphasized the stability and comfort of home and a home connected to others around the world and to creation. As a praise hymn and unsung ballad, the song takes on the timbre of joy as a declaration of good, lovable things in the world. As an anthem, "Tree Tree Tree" becomes energizing and motivating. The anthem for love extends outwards from the lover; it includes stuff in our houses, such as pillows and books, but also parts of creation, such as fish and trees. "Tree Tree Tree" roots us in a security in ourselves, homes, and world. Its message of love branches out to everyone and everything. The song inspires tremendous thanksgiving, contagious joy, and widespread praise.

Such praise is an action but, like all things in the world of *Mister Rogers' Neighborhood*, an action for children. It is not public policy or radical geoengineering projects. It is an extension of love that puts children in caring relationships with the world around them. It might seem to be a small thing. Nonetheless, as with Rogers's grown-up love of trees founded in his childhood experiences, these early affections are the small acorns that will grow into large trees. In other words, Rogers is not using his program to make activists but advocates; he encourages children to know they are loved so that they might love others. It is this foundation that will inspire children to care for the environment when they are grown so that they will not need to be activists. They will never even consider damaging the environment—or trees or fish or any other part of nature—because their love for creation has deep roots, all the way back to their childhood.

Conclusion

Fred Rogers and Environmental Wisdom

For children, care for the environment is rooted in play and exploration. This is the position of Angela Belli, the director of the Winnie Palmer Nature Preserve in Rogers's hometown of Latrobe, Pennsylvania. She and her staff run several programs for children where care and learning emerge from environmental play. On the grounds of the preserve are a barn, a pond, a garden, a bat house, a butterfly sanctuary, a hawk platform, countless trails, and a playground made out of the materials from the preserve. For programs at the center, ones that range from early childhood to school age children, there is usually a theme (like bugs or mammals), a story about the theme, an outdoor activity (like a hike or a game), and finally a craft. As a result, the center has resources for self-directed play for any child visiting the grounds and programs that get children thinking about and playing in nature.

Carin Vadala, Robert Bixler, and J. Joy James's research in "Childhood Play and Environmental Interests" backs up Belli's approach. They noted that when children have unstructured, self-directed play in the environment, they often turn elements of nature into toys. Trees become towers, sticks become swords, and so on. These kinds of interactions foster direct interest in the environment when children become adults. Then, they are more likely to discuss and act on environmental concerns. The researches also noted that structured outdoor play—like games, stories, and hikes—develop a fondness for nature. This kind of play is foundational for adults who are sympathetic to environmental concerns. In other words, the first type of play fosters actions, and the second type, affection.

In both cases, the idea is to get children into the environment and experience it for themselves. Doing so reshapes children's view of the environment. They see how plants and animals interact, and how the environment uses and reuses all things. Education centers like the Winnie Palmer Nature Preserve help children, as well as their adult caretakers, have positive encounters with the environment that foster action and affection for protecting the environment. Furthermore, educators often help children to come to see nature as everywhere, not just at the preserve, and so recommend caring and doing wherever they are. This can mean working to maintain the environment, but it can also mean doing small things in daily life. Children can pick up trash around their house, turn off lights, or stop using straws.

Even in 1990, Rogers grasped the need for affection and action in fostering care for the environment in children, putting him on the forefront of environmental education. The need for empathy and small acts is woven throughout the show, from seeing people connected to fish and puppets to reimagining things so they become toys and artwork and not trash. These principles are also on display in the booklet *Activities for Young Children about the Environment and Recycling* written by Fred Rogers with early childhood education experts Hedda Sharapan and Roberta Schomburg. The booklet was to be used with the Rogers's "Caring for the Environment" week, particularly Tuesday's episode with its visit to a recycling center. The booklet includes discussion topics, activities such as planting seeds, crafts with reused and natural materials, and recipes that use up leftover food. Addressing daycare providers and teachers, as well as parents and family, the booklet prioritizes both talking about feelings as well as directing children toward small actions and play that let them actualize those feelings and values.

The booklet, though, reveals another of Rogers's concerns. In it, children are asked "what would *they* do to solve the problem of having too much trash?" Clearly, this discussion happens with caring adults. However, this emphasis is passing, and the booklet sustains attention on artistic creation, some of which, after adults might explain the activity, allow children to play on their own. Rogers understood that the destruction of the natural world, that the piles of refuse in the home, that the trash filling up our own Someplace Elses can be overwhelming and exacerbate feelings of weakness and hopelessness as children understand their vulnerability and powerlessness. While he did propose activities children might do, in this booklet and during the week's episodes, he works to protect children from feeling threatened and insecure.

Hope and Trust

Daniel Tiger is not present in "Caring for the Environment." In fact, no child puppets are present. There is no Prince Tuesday; no Ana Platypus. Even the shy and nervous Henrietta Pussycat only appears once, caring for children at the factory while their parents work. The same is true of X the Owl, who, like Henrietta, seems to be a younger, yet adult puppet. While X is bothered by the oppressive nose muffs, he enthusiastically sets off to fly around the neighborhood looking for a new dump. However, we never hear from him again. Nor do we hear from Henrietta again as the catastrophe worsens and adult Make-Believe citizens worry and search for solutions.

Furthermore, school is suspended as teacher Harriet Elizabeth Cow must work with farmer Donkey Hodie to contain the mountain of trash. They build up fences to protect the school. Harriet Cow cannot leave the dump; she needs to work on the fence and keep the trash from overflowing. On Friday, she reveals how this work is taking its toll on her and her students when she states, "I'll be glad when I can get back to my fulltime teaching." While she has not withdrawn care, she cannot serve her students properly.

It's easy to see how ecophobia could develop in this make-believe situation. It is alienating to be afraid of one's home environment, of the living and nonliving things that crowd around us. Broader than germaphobia, ecophobia can grow a fear of one's home ecosystem into a pervasive anxiety about impending environmental disaster. These feelings can crop up, especially in a community that is full of trash where adults struggle to find solutions to environmental hazards. In the Neighborhood of Make-Believe drama, the trash apocalypse swiftly unfolds at the regional, even galactic, scale. It is easy to imagine Daniel Tiger's anxiety and horror were he included in the episode.

Ecophobia is the type of feeling that hurts the self deeply, and it also hurts the world. Rogers is clear and consistent in maintaining that children need ways of dealing with their anger, their fear, all their natural and healthy feelings, in ways that don't hurt themselves or anyone else. While building up children's confidence with adults in this series working together, he protects children when he makes the choice to leave out Daniel Tiger and the other young puppets in "Caring for the Environment."

Rogers understood that environmental disasters are complex and overwhelming. He did not visit an actual dump but a recycling center. He did not visit a polluted waterway but a healthy coral reef. Rogers was vocal about protecting children from television violence, whether in sitcoms or from the news. For example, in his famous 1968 special that addressed assassination, after the killings of Robert Kennedy and Martin Luther King Jr., Rogers spoke earnestly to parents in the context around watching television footage surrounding these events: "I plead for your protection and support of your young children. There is just so much that a very young child can take without it being overwhelming to him."

Beyond excluding Daniel Tiger, so that his anxiety would not overwhelm children, Rogers projects a world where neighbors band together and care for all things, including children. He speaks about this supreme and enabling trust in his Saint Vincent College commencement address from 2000, explaining, "What ultimately nourishes our souls is the knowing that we can be trusted, that we never have to fear the truth, that the foundation of our very being is good stuff." Because of this trust in ourselves and each other, Rogers also promises a good future. He repeatedly maintains that neighbors will love each other and love broadly, but he also reveals his deeply held belief that God has guaranteed our future. In his 1989 "Sermon for the Installation of the Reverend Kenneth L. Barley," he insists, "The only sure thing about anyone's future is that *God is already there.*" The way Rogers projects and affirms a connected world takes into account fear, anxiety, anger, and sadness, but it puts forward hope, affection, and action. His belief is not naïve; it is wise.

Environmental Wisdom

Wisdom is what children should gain from *Mister Rogers' Neighborhood*. Rogers's environmental wisdom is built on the ecological imagination Rogers promotes and reinforces in small actions children might perform in concert with their worldview. But it is also more than this. Wisdom includes imagination, knowledge, attitude, and behavior. Wisdom is a way of seeing processes, connections, and causes. Wisdom is a foresight and an insight. Wisdom requires honesty, authenticity, creativity, playfulness, depth, and applicability. Wisdom enables one to care for others and take care of one's self.

One can start developing wisdom at any age. Shea Tuttle, in her biography *Exactly as You Are*, describes Rogers himself as a wise child. In discussing the bullying young Rogers experienced as well as his response to those encounters, she explains, "Freddy—young, wise Freddy—took on the work of sadness on his own. He cried when he was alone—about the bullies, about his loneliness, about people's inability to see beyond the outside." Tuttle reminds us how

Rogers himself talked about his childhood experiences in a 1995 address at Saint Vincent College. Rogers remarked: "I started to look behind the things that people did and said. [. . .] So after a lot of sadness, I began a lifelong search for what is essential, what it is about my neighbor that doesn't meet the eye."

In Rogers's own words, this is what wisdom can do: it can help us find the "essential [that] is invisible" in each other. Ecological imagination stretches the mind to see connections among each piece, part, material, being, creature, community, organization, and neighborhood as interacting and entangled. The purpose of Fred Rogers's ecological imagination is not to inspire children to accomplish small acts, although that activism can be helpful and nurturing. Rather, Rogers's ecological imagination helps children grow on their invisible insides, encouraging them to be wise.

The first piece of Rogers's wisdom is hope. He uses *Mister Rogers' Neighborhood* to show a world of possibilities. In "Caring for the Environment," he does not gloss over the challenges and consequences of environmental issues but he also does not try to frighten children with the crisis. Instead, he shows possibilities, even in the face of overwhelming problems. Hope motivates one to care for the self and for others. From the perspective of a hopeful world, Rogers reveals how all creatures and things are interconnected. His interspecies puppet neighbors, the real fish and goats near and far, the homemade toys and artwork—all these are connected to each other in a system of circulating love. This second realization is the next piece of Rogers's wisdom: hope makes it easier to build relationships of affection.

Rogers's third piece of wisdom pivots between feeling and action. Rogers asks us to look for helpers and become helpers. His television program repeatedly expresses that no one is alone and no one has all the answers. Together, though, we are sacred and strong. In "Caring for the Environment," Rogers shows children that they can recycle their ideas as they reuse household scraps, collect and sort recyclables, and care for their pets and toys. He shows adults talking and working together to care for their neighbors and their world. In particular, Rogers makes clear that adults help by cultivating a protected space for children that is supported and sustained.

In moving from hope to affectionate relationships to helping action, Rogers builds a world that drives, expands, and enacts care. His ecological wisdom provides an imaginative framework, spiritual nourishment, and giving attitude that can help us access insight and buttress foresight. Wisdom is an invisible essential for being a good neighbor to all of creation, and Rogers cultivates the ground for such environmental wisdom to grow.

Appendix

"Caring for the Environment"

Episode Summaries

Monday—Episode 1616: Reduce, Reuse, Recycle
After the opening song, "It's Such a Good Feeling," Mister Rogers shows viewers a greeting card with a picture of a fish on it. He shows how you can recycle it by turning it into a post card to send to someone new. When Mr. McFeely shows up, Mister Rogers shows him the new card. Mr. McFeely likes it, saying, "You like to save things too!" and then, "I hate to waste anything." He then shows Mister Rogers how he recycles paper and uses it to make notepads for his delivery business and his grandchildren. He then tells Mister Rogers he worries about the dump that has grown into a "mountain" and how he is determined to do something about it. Just before Mr. McFeely departs, he tells Mister Rogers, "Before you throw anything out, just think . . . and don't buy anything you don't really need." After saying goodbye to Mr. McFeely, Mister Rogers sees a paper bag in his yard and brings it in. He decides not to throw it away but to "think" of something to do with it. Trolley then takes viewers to the Neighborhood of Make-Believe.

It is garbage day in the neighborhood, and Handyman Negri is collecting trash. He tells Trolley that there is more trash each year.

Handyman Negri's garbage collection is interrupted by King Friday who wants to play music with him. When King Friday hands him the music, Handyman Negri wonders why there are so many sheets. King Friday says, "Well, when I asked for two, the copier made 200. You'll just have to throw the 198 away." After the duet, Bob Dog shows up. He notes how much garbage there is and says that "people sure throw a lot of things away." Then, Mr. McFeely arrives and asks if he can have the extra paper since he is trying to save everything. He then tells Handyman Negri that the dump at Someplace Else is almost full. Handyman Negri is surprised, saying he's never heard of a dump getting full before. Bob Dog says we should, "think before throwing anything away." Handyman Negri decides to check out the dump before taking over all the garbage. Bob Dog goes to collect more garbage, telling Mr. McFeely he will save what he can. When he arrives at the Museum-Go-Around, Lady Elaine throws out lots of trash, telling Bob Dog not to worry as there is always room at the dump. When Handyman Negri arrives at the dump, he finds Harriet Elizabeth Cow and Donkey Hodie completing a fence to keep the trash from overtaking the school and farm. They tell Handyman Negri he will have to find a new dump for the garbage, so Handyman Negri returns to the castle to tell King Friday and Queen Sara about the situation. They are in a meeting, so Bob Dog and Handyman Negri decide to wait for them. While they are waiting they notice that the garbage is starting to smell.

Upon Trolley's return, Mister Rogers says he didn't remember the dump being at Someplace Else and "I guess we don't think about things like dumps until we can't use them anymore." Mister Rogers tells viewers that, next time, they will make believe about what they will do about the garbage. Then, Mister Rogers says he thought of something to do with the paper bag he found. He grabs some balls and goes outside to play the "Bag Ball Game." He tries to roll the balls into the bag. While he is doing it, Marilyn Barnett, a physical education teacher and neighbor, shows up and leads Mister Rogers in exercises. Toward the end, Marilyn shows Mister Rogers how to make himself into a ball to stretch his back. Mister Rogers then shows Marilyn his bag ball game. When she rolls a ball into the bag, the bag tips up, and Mister Rogers says, "Oh, you got it to stand up!" Mister Rogers then asks Marilyn if she has any ideas for using the bag, and she says it could be used as a trash bag or a bag to hold things.

Mister Rogers then goes inside. He echoes Mr. McFeely's thought that you should think before you throw anything away and don't buy anything you don't need. Mister Rogers says this is a way we can all help. He then reminds viewers of everything they did that day. Just before the episode ends, Mister Rogers asks his viewers, "Do you know what recycling means? Well, if you want to know, ask someone you know. And, next time we are together, we can talk about it."

Tuesday—1617: A Visit to a Recycling Center
When Mister Rogers enters, he is carrying the paper bag from the day before, but it is filled up. He asks his viewers to guess what is inside. He says, it is "not balls, not an elephant, not the dining room table. I'll tell you. Some cans and glass bottles." Mister Rogers says people have thrown them away because they are done with them. However, he says that "there's one more thing we can do with them. We can help them get recycled." He says Mr. McFeely will take them to the recycling center on this day. While waiting for Mr. McFeely, Mister Rogers feeds the fish and sings the song "I Like to Take Care of You." He pauses in the middle of the song to ask viewers to think about what they take care of. When Mr. McFeely arrives, he helps Mister Rogers sort the cans and bottles in the paper bag into separate boxes to prepare for the recycling center. Then, they both walk to the recycling center.

When they arrive, a worker named Bob greets them and says they should put their recycling material on the scale to be weighed. After asking if it is OK, Mister Rogers gets on the scale himself. Bob then takes Mister Rogers and Mr. McFeely to watch the process of recycling cans. They put on safety goggles and watch as the cans are put into the compressor and crushed. Bob explains that they will ship this material to places where they will make new cans. Bob then shows them cardboard and plastic that have gone through the same process as the cans. Then, they watch as glass is ground down into smaller bits and prepared for recycling. After returning from the recycling center, Mister Rogers tells his viewers that it is nice to know things can be reused, we shouldn't waste things, and we shouldn't use more than we need. This sets up a trip to the Neighborhood of Make-Believe.

When Trolley arrives in the Neighborhood of Make-Believe, he finds Miss Paulificate wearing a nose muff so that she doesn't have to smell the trash. After Trolley leaves, Lady Aberlin arrives. She is also wearing a nose muff. King Friday then emerges and gives Lady Aberlin the assignment of finding a new dump. Lady Aberlin starts her assignment by visiting X the Owl. X the Owl wants to try on the nose muff, but, when he does, he dislikes it, saying he cannot breathe. He agrees to help by flying around and looking for a new dump. Lady Aberlin then visits the factory. Hilda Dingleboarder tells her that the factory has stopped making rocking chairs and is instead making nose muffs. Before going back into the factory, Hilda says she wishes people would recycle. Next, Cornflake S. Pecially (Corny) comes out of the factory and gives Lady Aberlin scraps of wood to be thrown away. When Lady Aberlin says that the dump is full, Corny suggests using the dump at Westwood. After Corny leaves, Henriette Pussycat emerges. She is watching the children at the factory and thinks Corny's idea of using Westwood's dump is a good idea. Lady Aberlin goes to the castle to suggest to King Friday that they should use Westwood's dump. When she gets to the castle though, Mayor Maggie from Westwood arrives for an emergency meeting with King Friday. She tells the king that her dump is full too and was wondering if Westwood could use the dump at Someplace Else. Lady Aberlin and Miss Paulificate tell Mayor Maggie that their dump is full as well. Trolley arrives and takes the viewers back to Mister Rogers's house. Back at the house, Mister Rogers takes out some wooden blocks, made by a friend from wood that was going to be thrown away.

Mister Rogers says the idea with blocks is to "build one building and then use the same blocks to build another building." He continues, saying, "That is recycling right there—use the same thing over to do something else." All that is required, Rogers emphasizes, is imagination. Rogers then goes and gets cardboard tubes and tissue paper to make trees. He says it is an idea he got from one of his teachers. He says, "You know, the best kind of toy is the one you make for yourself. When you make things for yourself, it's like taking care of yourself." Then Mister Rogers sings "I Like to Take Care of You" and transitions to "It's Such a Good Feeling" to end the episode.

Wednesday—1618: Caring for Our Planet by Recycling
The episode begins with Mister Rogers showing his viewers a puzzle made from a piece of wood that "someone was going to throw away." He takes it into the kitchen and disassembles it. The wooden block puzzle has several pieces, and pieces within pieces. Mister Rogers says it has "secret" parts and is beautiful. This reminds him of a time he visited Mrs. McFeely, who made several things out of material that was going to be thrown away. The show then flashes back to this previous episode.

In the flashback, Mrs. McFeely shows Mister Rogers how she made a bird feeder from a milk carton and dowel rod. Then she shows Mister Rogers a pillow she made from an old sheet. Finally, she shows Mister Rogers a rug she and her friends made out of old wool clothes. She ends by saying, "There's lots of things you can do with old things."

When Mister Rogers returns to the present, he says, "memories are things that you can use over and over again." When Mr. McFeely arrives, he brings Mister Rogers a video recording of a visit to Leo Sewell who makes "sculptures out of thrown-away things." As they watch the video, Mr. McFeely tells Mister Rogers that, as a child, Leo collected thrown-out things and liked to work in his dad's woodworking shop. As an adult, Leo had the idea of putting these two interests together to make sculptures. Mr. McFeely and Mister

Rogers note how Leo collects material from people who are getting rid of it, organizes the material in different locations throughout the studio, and thinks carefully about what material to use in his sculptures. In the video, Mr. McFeely stops to look at a large sculpture of a fish, a marlin, that is hanging on the wall. Mister Rogers notes how Leo takes old things and makes them new through his art. As the video ends, Mister Rogers says, "People can do so much with their imagination."

After the video is over and Mr. McFeely leaves for more speedy deliveries, Trolley takes the viewer to the Neighborhood of Make-Believe. Trolley arrives to find Handyman Negri fanning the smell of the trash up in the air. When Mayor Maggie shows up, they note that the fanning is helping but is not a permanent solution. Mayor Maggie tells Handyman Negri that she and King Friday are going to look for another dump but that, in the meantime, she needs to return to Westwood "to see how our people and animals are faring." Lady Aberlin then proceeds to Lady Elaine's Museum-Go-Around. Lady Elaine suggests putting the trash in an airplane and sending it to Just Anywhere. Lady Aberlin suggests that Just Anywhere might not want it. She then asks Lady Elaine to call Betty Templeton in Southwood to see if the Neighborhood of Make-Believe and Westwood can use their dump. However, when Lady Elaine speaks to Betty on the phone, she finds out that the dump in Southwood is also full. Lady Elaine then tells Lady Aberlin that their last hope is "Old Goat in Northwood." Handyman Negri then calls and tells them that Old Goat and another goat are already on their way to the castle. As Lady Aberlin returns to the castle, she stops and sees Hilda Dingleboarder, who is working on something to do with trash. They both express hope that something will solve the garbage problem. When Lady Aberlin gets back to the castle, King Friday appears and give Handyman Negri a mechanical fan to help with the smell, and Lady Aberlin tells the king that the goats from Northwood are on their way. As Trolley takes the viewers back to Mister Rogers's neighborhood, everyone in Make-Believe can be heard saying, "We are all in this together."

Back at Mister Rogers house, he sings "You are Special" as he moves back to the kitchen where the wood block puzzle is still disassembled on the table. Mister Rogers plays a quick game of peekaboo and then says the puzzle is too difficult for him to put back together himself. He says he is going to ask a friend and "it's a good feeling that you don't have to solve everything by yourself." The episode ends with Mister Rogers singing "It's Such a Good Feeling."

Thursday—1619: Snorkeling with Sylvia Earle
The episode begins with Mister Rogers showing his viewers equipment for snorkeling, including fins (which he plays peekaboo behind), water skin (wetsuit), mask, and snorkel. He tells viewers he likes to remember the time he went snorkeling with marine biologists Sylvia Earle. The show then cuts to Mister Rogers's field trip to the ocean and coral reef.

The sequence begins with Mister Rogers and Sylvia Earle on a boat, named the *Infante*, heading out into the ocean. Before entering the water, Mister Rogers asks Sylvia if she liked the water as a child. She said she loved it and, "like most young things, I was curious." She said her parents let her explore and come to know fish "on their own terms." Mister Rogers replies by saying, "And those creatures are probably just as curious about us as we are about them." Sylvia agrees and says that he'll see this when the two of them go to the fish's "neighborhood." They then dive into the water and swim around the coral reef, observing the plants and fish while music accompanies them. Mister Rogers pauses in the middle of the swim to ask Sylvia the names of some of the fish and then to proclaim that it is "a beautiful day in this neighborhood." After they finish snorkeling, Mister Rogers asks Sylvia what can be done to take care of places like the coral reef. Sylvia replies, "Well, one of the important things is to do what we were doing, to get out and know the place. It's hard to care about something if you don't understand it, if you haven't seen it. So being in the sea is an important step in the right direction. Get to know the fish. Get to see the coral and understand how they live. When they do, it's hard not to care about them." She also notes how the ocean is important for all of us, generating the oxygen that we need. She concludes by saying that it is "just part good, common sense to take care of this ocean that, in its own way, has taken care of us."

Upon returning to the neighborhood, Mister Rogers says that people like Sylvia are his heroes because they keep the world safe for everybody and care about the world. Mister Rogers then shows his viewers photographs of French, queen, and gray angelfish, noting that they are all angelfish even though they look different. He then sings the song "Did You Know?," a song on wondering about things. Mister Rogers finishes by saying that there is a real world under the sea and that it is important to take care of it, "very important." He then calls the Trolley to take viewers to the Neighborhood of Make-Believe.

In the Neighborhood of Make-Believe, Lady Aberlin is operating the mechanical fan to get rid of the trash smell. Old Goat and New Goat arrive from Northwood, but they are so tired from their trip they immediately take a nap. Lady Elaine then appears in the castle and says she has two good ideas for taking care of the trash. First, she suggests throwing it into the ocean. Lady Aberlin says that won't work as it will just fill up the ocean like it did Someplace Else. Second, Lady Elaine suggests going on the television show *The Universe Today* and talking to Patrice, the host of the show and Lady Elaine's friend. When King Friday arrives, he affirms Lady Elaine's idea to go on television and prepares the "purple jet" to take both him and Lady Elaine to the show. Then, Neighbor Aber arrives wearing a wetsuit. He says that he has checked out the oceans but that they are just "too beautiful to dump things into." The Goats then wake up and ask for a snack, but, before anyone can get them something to eat, Miss Paulificate arrives with a television set to watch *The Universe Today*. The Trolley arrives and takes viewers back to Mister Rogers's neighborhood.

After the Trolley returns, Mister Rogers asks his viewers what they think will happen. He also says, "One thing's sure, everybody seems to be trying to help, somehow." He then goes to feed his fish and shows viewers that there is an angelfish in his fish tank. He says the fish live in the water, it is their home, and no one wants garbage dumped in their home. He then says fish are fancy, just like every person, and sings "Everybody's Fancy." After the song, he says each animal is fancy, and, if we find out what is fine about them, we will want to take care of them. He then sings the concluding song, "It's Such a Good Feeling."

Friday—1620: Making Toys from Throw-Aways
Mister Rogers brings in a box filled with objects. He takes them to the kitchen to show his viewers. The first item is a box with a hole cut in it, so it looks like a television set. He then tapes some bottle tops onto the box to look like knobs. He says, "These are things that might have been thrown away but weren't." Then, Mister Rogers makes two puppets out of handkerchiefs and balls. Finally, he puts the puppets, named Charlie and George, in the television set to put on a show where the two puppets sing. At this time, Mr. McFeely shows up.

Mr. McFeely stopped by Mister Roger's house with a goat that he is taking to show the children at the neighborhood school. The goat is named William. Mr. McFeely tells Mister Rogers that William is hungry, and Mister Rogers asks if he can eat anything, like cans or trash. Mr. McFeely says, "That's not true. He doesn't eat just anything. That's not true. He likes nuts, and grains, and he likes vegetables ... they're very particular about what they eat." Mister Rogers notes that William is a vegetarian. Mister Rogers then feeds him some carrots. Before Mr. McFeely leaves, he gives Mister Rogers a shoe box that, instead of being thrown away, has been made to look like Trolley by Mrs. McFeely. Mister Rogers takes the cardboard Trolley inside and then uses it to take viewers to the Neighborhood of Make-Believe.

In the Neighborhood of Make-Believe, Lady Aberlin and Queen Sara are talking about the garbage problem. Queen Sara hopes that something will come from King Friday's appearance on *The Universe Today*, and Lady Aberlin hopes for some idea from the goats, commenting that maybe that they will eat all the garbage. Meanwhile, Old Goat and New Goat have gone to Someplace Else to visit the dump. Lady Aberlin goes to the dump to see them. On her way, she runs into Neighbor Aber. He tells her that the goats have been visiting all the dumps to check out the problem. When she tells him that she thought the goats might eat all the garbage, Neighbor Abor says, "Goats don't eat garbage. Somebody made that up about goats. In fact, goats are very picky." Together then, they go to the dump. When they arrive, New Goat and Old Goat are asking Harriet Cow and Donkey Hodie about the trash, wondering if they have plastic, glass, and metal in their dump. When Neighbor Aber and Lady Aberlin ask the goats what they are going to do, they say they might be able to solve the garbage problem not only in the Neighborhood of Make-Believe but also in Southwood and Westwood. However, Old Goat and New Goat first need a fax machine to contact their colleagues back in Northwood. They send a fax, and, while they are waiting for a reply, *The Universe Today* comes on, with Patrice interviewing Lady Elaine and King Friday. Lady Elaine explains the problem and says she proposed dumping the garbage into the ocean, but Patrice says, "Well, the fish probably would have had some thoughts on that, too." King Friday comes on after Lady Elaine. After Patrice tells him they need to discuss the crisis before he plays his bass violin, they take callers. The first caller says that there should be solutions other than finding new dumps. The second caller says that King Friday is one cool dude. The third caller is Sue Goat from Northwood who says that she is working with Old Goat and New Goat and they will help solve the garbage problem. They will "divide and conquer" by dividing up the garbage into different types so that it can be recycled. Mrs. Dingleboarder suddenly appears, causing King Friday to ask her if she knows where she is. She says she can help and shows Patrice her invention, which takes a piece of garbage and turns it into something useful. She demonstrates it by having Patrice put a wad of paper in the machine. The paper is turned into a fan, and, when the fan is put in, the machine turns it into a row of crowns. Patrice ends the show saying, "So you see, folks, sometimes, the solution to many problems can be found right next door." King Friday adds that the goats will divide the garbage, Mrs. Dingleboarder's machine will do the rest, and he will play his bass violin. Back at the castle, everyone is happy with the solution. Mayor Maggie says, "We all got together and solved another problem," and Neighbor Aber adds, "That is what neighbors are meant to do."

Back at Mister Rogers's house, he emphasizes that help is often very close by, it is important to ask for help, and you should work to help yourself. He then takes the cardboard Trolley to the kitchen where he left the cardboard television and homemade puppets. He then plays with the puppets and says you can make up games and play with anything around the house. It is something you can be proud of doing. He then sings "I'm Proud of You" and ends the show with "It's Such a Good Feeling."

Acknowledgments

There are so many neighbors we would like to thank.

The Fred Rogers Center

We are honored to be recognized as Fred Rogers Faculty Fellows from the Fred Rogers Center. Former codirectors over the years, including Junlei Li, Rita Catalano, Maxwell King, and Roberta Schomburg, have been supportive, as have faculty Dana Winters and Jeremy Boyle, who always had time to discuss Fred. Conversations with Jeremy helped to frame Fred's artistry. Conversations with Dana, now the director of the Fred Rogers Center, propelled events and collaborations. The way Junlei talks about Fred Rogers—the earnest intellectual inquiry, the depth of his understanding, and his recognition of Fred's heights—deepened our appreciation for Fred's work and broadened our confidence in his status as a public intellectual. Archivist Emily Uhrin has been a singular guide through the Fred Rogers Archives.

Saint Vincent College

The thinking in this book was advanced by many conversations and extra eyes on the manuscript. Chris McMahon offers continual support as the chair of theology, as does Margaret Watkins, the dean of the School of Arts, Humanities, and Social Sciences, and John Smetanka, the vice president for academic affairs. Eric and Holly Mohr, of *Mister Rogers and Philosophy*, have advanced so many conversations and events to deepen our understanding of Fred's philosophical bent. Julia Snyder and Sophie Neubert provided administrative assistance with diligence and competence.

I (Sara) would like to express particular gratitude for the many conversations with Patricia Sharbaugh. Patty's insight, wisdom, and compassion have made her invaluable to me and this book. I also benefited from an inspirational discussion about doxology with Luke Briola. Jessica Harvey, Michelle Gil-Montero, Dennis McDaniel, and Clare Beams have talked about this book with me, and I am grateful for their comradery and friendship. My colleagues Sara Hart and Devin Fava have kept me grounded these last few years. And I'd like to acknowledge Tina Johnson and Kimberly Baker for their early support of my research and writing. My former students inspire me with their intelligence, kindness, grit, and heart, some of whom are Rachel Maley, Kylie McGinnis, Zach Tackett, Joe Carroll, Mallory Truckenmiller, Kaitlyn Thomas, and Sophia Sommers.

Friends and Family

I (Sara) have been so fortunate to have deep friendships, and these are the people who I leaned on while working on this book: Lisa Christian, Kelly Stange, Kate Gorman, Jamey Leonard, Calvin Li, Chris Mathyssek, Joe Bielevicz, Rebecca Thurston, Kathryn Roecklein, Lisa Donofrio, Jeff Rothman, Kirk Erikson, Ana Rodríguez, Matt Allen, Mariss Mednis, Casey O'Hara, and my fellow readers, Beth Praire, Kristin Udvari, Elaine Musgrave, Judith Yanowitz, and Maureen May. Emily Braham has been family to my children, spending six years of Saturday nights with them. Thank you also to the teachers at Linda Stagon's Edgewood Daycare and Pittsburgh Public's Colfax K-8. Friends are family. And, yet, of course, my family: my parents, Ron and Joan Berrey, instilled a belief in me of my own powers (and also put on *Mister Rogers' Neighborhood*). My love extends to my late brother, Daniel C. Berrey; my brother, Ben Berrey; my coparent, Dan Lindey; and, most of all, our curious, kind, imaginative, smart, loving, and lovable children, Pete and Andy.

I (Jason) would like to thank my wife, Kelly, for supporting me throughout this project.

Notes

Introduction: Fred Rogers's Ecological Imagination

3 **Walt Whitman's poetry**: Walt Whitman, *Leaves of Grass: The First (1855) Edition*. New York: Penguin Books, 2005 (1855).

3 **"you don't need to binge-watch"**: Gavin Edwards, *Kindness and Wonder: Why Mister Rogers Matters Now More Than Ever* (New York: Harper Collins, 2019), 7.

4 **At the moment you are reading this book**: Ibid., 6.

4 **10 percent of American households!**: Maxwell King, *The Good Neighbor: The Life and Work of Fred Rogers* (New York: Abrams, 2018), 355.

5 **"First, [Rogers] recognized"**: Ibid., 235.

6 **he demands quality television**: Fred Rogers, "Invisible to the Eye: Johnson & Johnson Speech" (Latrobe, PA: Fred Rogers Archives, 1994), 2.

6 **"He didn't *teach* about clay"**: Ibid., 2.

6 **celebrate Aunt Bert's life**: Ibid., 5.

7 **"radical Christian pacifist"**: Michael Long, *Peaceful Neighbor: Discovering the Countercultural Mister Rogers* (Louisville, KY: Westminster John Knox Press, 2015), xvii, xii.

7 **"a God who accepts us"**: Ibid., xxi.

7 **"L'essentiel est invisible"**: Antoine de Saint-Exupéry, *The Little Prince*, trans. Richard Howard (Boston: Mariner Books, 2000), 63.

8 **"On the walls of our Family Communications offices"**: Fred Rogers, "National Association for the Education of Young Children" (Latrobe, PA: Fred Rogers Archives, 1993); Fred Rogers, "Invisible to the Eye: Johnson & Johnson Speech" (Latrobe, PA: Fred Rogers Archives, 1994).

9 **the famous 1969 Senate hearing**: Fred Rogers, "Senate Hearings on Public Broadcasting" (Latrobe, PA: Fred Rogers Archives, 1969).

10	**"the true meaning of love"**: Fred Rogers, "Encouraging Creativity: Theil College Commencement Address" (Latrobe, PA: Fred Rogers Archives, 1969).
10	**"May this theological seminary"**: Fred Rogers, "Invisible Essentials: Memphis Theological Seminary Address" (Latrobe, PA: Fred Rogers Archives, 1997).
11	**In this monumental lecture**: Ibid.
11	**"love-ethic"**: William Guy, "The Theology of *Mister Rogers' Neighborhood*," in *Mister Rogers Neighborhood: Children Television and Fred Rogers*, eds. Mark Collins and Margaret Mary Kimmel (Pittsburgh: University of Pittsburgh Press, 1996), 106.
11	**"Paradoxically one *can* have it all"**: Ibid., 118.
12	**"What I've come to understand"**: Fred Rogers, "Commencement Address for Saint Vincent College" (Latrobe, PA: Fred Rogers Archives, 1989), 1–8.
12	**"I feel the closer we get"**: Ibid., 1.
12	**"an invisible gift"**: Ibid., 6.
12	**"in the midst of this community"**: Ibid., 8.
13	**"the freedom to see life as providing good feelings"**: Guy, 10.
14	**"the Christian pastoral"**: Chris Buczinsky, "The Performance of the Pastoral," in *Revisiting Mister Rogers' Neighborhood: Essays on Lessons About Self and Community*, eds. Kathy Merlock Jackson and Steven M. Emmanuel (Jefferson, NC: McFarland and Company, 2015), 3.
15	**"scarcity, recycling, and conservation"**: Fred Rogers, Hedda Sharapan, and Roberta Schomburg, "Activities for Young Children About the Environment and Recycling" (Pittsburgh: Family Communications, 1990), 1.
16	**"environmental justice poetics"**: Kamala Platt, "Environmental Justice Children's Literature: Depicting, Defending, and Celebrating Trees and Birds, Colors and People," in *Wild Things: Children's Culture and Ecocriticism*, eds. Sidney I. Dobrin and Kenneth B. Kidd (Detroit: Wayne State University Press, 2004), 184.
16	**"children are naturally closer to nature"**: Sidney I. Dobrin and Kenneth B. Kidd, "Introduction: Into the Wild," in *Wild Things: Children's Culture and Ecocriticism*, eds. Sidney I. Dobrin and Kenneth B. Kidd (Detroit: Wayne State University Press, 2004), 7.

Chapter One: Make-Believe and Reality: Rogers's Apocalyptic Environmentalism

21	**"do you know where you are?"**: *Mister Rogers' Neighborhood*, #1620, "Caring for the Environment: Making Toys from Throw-Aways," performed by Fred Rogers, aired April 20, 1990, PBS.
22	**"ecophobia"**: Susan Jean Strife, "Children's Environmental Concerns: Expressing Ecophobia," *Journal of Environmental Education* 43, no. 1 (2012): 38, 42, 50.

22	**doom-and-destruction**: Clare Echterling, "How to Save the World and Other Lessons from Children's Environmental Literature," *Children's Literature in Education* 47, no. 4 (2016): 283–99.
24	**the dump is full**: *Mister Rogers' Neighborhood*, #1616, "Caring for the Environment: Reduce, Reuse, Recycle," performed by Fred Rogers, aired April 16, 1990, PBS.
25	**a national sacrifice zone**: Rebecca Scott, *Removing Mountains: Extracting Nature and Identity in the Appalachia Coalfields* (Minneapolis: University of Minnesota Press, 2010), 31–64.
25	**"toxic consciousness"**: Cynthia Deitering, "The Postnatural Novel: Toxic Consciousness in Fiction of the 1980s," in *The Ecocriticism Reader: Landmarks in Literary Ecology*, eds. Cheryll Glotfelty and Harold Fromm (Athens: University of Georgia Press, 1996), 197.
26	**"slow violence"**: Rob Nixon, *Slow Violence and the Environmentalism of the Poor* (Cambridge: Harvard University Press, 2011).
26	**"I cant breathe"**: *Mister Rogers Neighborhood*, #1617, "Caring for the Environment: A Visit to a Recycling Center," performed by Fred Rogers, aired April 17, 1990, PBS.
28	**"the little quiet moments"**: Fred Rogers, "Sermon for Installation of the Reverend Kenneth Barley" (Latrobe, PA: Fred Rogers Archives, 1989), 2.
29	**"The whole universe"**: *Mister Rogers' Neighborhood*, #1619, "Caring for the Environment: Snorkeling with Sylvia Earle," performed by Fred Rogers, aired April 19, 1990, PBS.
30	**mutual interdependency in a public space**: Matthew Ussia, "Mister Rogers's Lessons for Democracy," in *Mister Rogers and Philosophy: Wondering Through the Neighborhood*, eds. Eric J. Mohr and Holly K. Mohr (Chicago: Open Court, 2020), 185, 186, 188, 189.
30	**"for the time being"**: *Mister Rogers' Neighborhood*, #1618, "Caring for the Environment: Caring for our Planet by Recycling," performed by Fred Rogers, aired April 18, 1990, PBS.
30	**"anything can happen"**: *Mister Rogers' Neighborhood*, #1619, "Caring for the Environment: Snorkeling with Sylvia Earle," performed by Fred Rogers, aired April 19, 1990, PBS.
31	**"How natural!"**: *Mister Rogers' Neighborhood*, #1620, "Caring for the Environment: Making Toys from Throw-Aways," performed by Fred Rogers, aired April 20, 1990, PBS.
31	**"inherently imaginative"**: Timothy Gilmore, "After the Apocalypse: Wildness as Preservative in a Time of Ecological Crisis," *ISLE: Interdisciplinary Studies in Literature and Environment* 24, no. 3 (2017): 391, 392, 408.
32	**the coming apocalyptic "end"**: Micha Kiel, *Apocalyptic Ecology: The Book of Revelation, the Earth, and the Future* (Minnesota: Liturgical Press, 2017), 115–22.

34	**"We're all in this together!"**: *Mister Rogers' Neighborhood*, #1618, "Caring for the Environment: Caring for our Planet by Recycling," performed by Fred Rogers, aired April 18, 1990, PBS.
35	**a fax-machine**: *Mister Rogers' Neighborhood*, #1620, "Caring for the Environment: Making Toys from Throw-Aways," performed by Fred Rogers, aired April 20, 1990, PBS.
36	**Parents inculcate wonder**: Ann Pelo, "A Sense of Wonder: Cultivating an Ecological Identity in Young Children—and in Ourselves," *Canadian Children* 39, no. 2 (2014): 5–8.
36	**"our attitude"**: Fred Rogers, "Caring for Our Planet: Care That's Caught" (Latrobe, PA: Fred Rogers Archives, 1990), 2.
36	**Rogers articulates**: Fred Rogers, "Commencement Address for Saint Vincent College" (Latrobe, PA: Fred Rogers Archives, 1989), 18.
37	**the biblical apocalyptic tradition**: Robin Veldman, "Narrating the Environmental Apocalypse," *Ethics & the Environment* 17, no. 1 (2012): 5.
38	**"take the time"**: *Mister Rogers' Neighborhood*, #1205, performed by Fred Rogers, aired March 3, 1972, PBS.
38	**"memories are things"**: *Mister Rogers' Neighborhood*, #1618, "Caring for the Environment: Caring for our Planet by Recycling," performed by Fred Rogers, aired April 18, 1990, PBS.
38	**children become overwhelmed**: Glynne Mackey, "To Know, To Decide, To Act: The Young Child's Right to Participate in Action for the Environment," *Environmental Education Research* 18, no. 4 (2012): 474.
39	**child's agency**: Ibid., 482.
39	**the choices of children**: J. Joy James and Robert D. Bixler, "Children's Role in Meaning Making Through Their Participation in an Environmental Education Program," *Journal of Environmental Education* 39, no. 4 (2008): 44–59, 56–58.
39	**"more opportunities to engage"**: Strife, "Children's Environmental Concerns," 50, 51.
41	**use organic dye**: *Mister Rogers' Neighborhood*, #1205, performed by Fred Rogers, aired March 3, 1972, PBS, retrieved via Daily Motion, https://www.dailymotion.com/video/x5rboup.
42	**"free space"**: Susan Larkin, "Fantasy as Free-Space: Mister Rogers' Neighborhoods," in *Revisiting* Mister Rogers' Neighborhood: *Essays on Lessons About Self and Community*, eds. Kathy Merlock Jackson and Steven M. Emmanuel (Jefferson, NC: McFarland and Company, 2016), 77, 82.

Chapter Two: The Art of Environmentalism: Integral Ecology in Fred Rogers's Neighborhoods

43	**a greeting card**: *Mister Rogers' Neighborhood*, #1616, "Caring for the Environment: Reduce, Reuse, Recycle," performed by Fred Rogers, aired April 16, 1990, PBS.

45 **"the creative artist"**: Fred Rogers. "Encouraging Creativity: Theil College Commencement Address" (Latrobe, PA: Fred Rogers Archives, 1969).

45 **philosophy of art**: David Boersema, "The Virtues of Art," in *Mister Rogers and Philosophy: Wondering Through the Neighborhood*, eds. Eric J. Mohr and Holly K. Mohr (Chicago: Open Court, 2020), 69, 71, 75, 72, 73.

46 **sculptor Leo Sewell's studio**: *Mister Rogers' Neighborhood*, #1618, "Caring for the Environment: Caring for our Planet by Recycling," performed by Fred Rogers, aired April 18, 1990, PBS.

47 **the coral reef**: *Mister Rogers' Neighborhood*, #1619, "Caring for the Environment: Snorkeling with Sylvia Earle," performed by Fred Rogers, aired April 19, 1990, PBS.

49 **ocean ecosystems**: Nicole Starosielski. "Beyond Fluidity: A Cultural History of Cinema Under Water," in *Ecocinema Theory and Practice*, eds. Stephen Rust, Salma Monani, and Sean Cubitt (New York: Routledge, 2013), 165.

50 **"disquieting picture books"**: Jessica Whitelaw, "Beyond the Bedtime Story: In Search of Epistemic Possibilities and the Innovative Potential of Disquieting Picturebooks," *Bookbird: A Journal of International Children's Literature* 55, no. 1 (2017): 37, 39.

53 **"sacred art"**: Carol Zaleski, "Mister Rogers," *Christian Century*, April 19, 2003, 35.

53 **"environmental ethics"**: Chris Buczinsky, "The Performance of the Pastoral," in *Revisiting Mister Rogers' Neighborhood: Essays on Lessons About Self and Community*, eds. Kathy Merlock Jackson and Steven M. Emmanuel (Jefferson, NC: McFarland and Company, 2015), 9.

54 **"integral ecology"**: Francis, *Laudato Sí* (Washington, DC: United States Conference of Catholic Bishops, 2015), 10.

54 **"ecological commitments"**: Ibid., 64, 70.

54 **"overcome reductionism"**: Ibid., 112.

59 **turn them into puppets**: *Mister Rogers' Neighborhood*, #1620, "Caring for the Environment: Making Toys from Throw-Aways," performed by Fred Rogers, aired April 20, 1990, PBS.

61 **"prosocial values"**: Kathy Merlock Jackson, "Social Activism for the Small Set," in *Revisiting Mister Rogers' Neighborhood: Essays on Lessons About Self and Community*, eds. Kathy Merlock Jackson and Steven M. Emmanuel (Jefferson, NC: McFarland and Company, 2015), 14, 13.

61 **"liveliness hidden in such things"**: Jane Bennett, "Systems and Things: On Vital Materialism and Object-Oriented Philosophy," in *The Nonhuman Turn*, ed. Richard Grusin (Minneapolis: University of Minnesota Press, 2015), 235.

Chapter Three: Puppets and Animal Wisdom: Ecological Conversion

64 **"my *friend* had come in need"**: Fred Rogers, "More Than We Know," principal address at the Opening Ceremonies of the Sesquicentennial of Saint Vincent, Saint Vincent Archabbey Basilica (Latrobe, PA: Fred Rogers Archives, 1995), 2–3.

65 **"ecological conversion"**: Francis, *Laudato Sí*, 216, 218, 219, 220, 221, 92.

66 **protest fur sales**: Michael Long, *Peaceful Neighbor: Discovering the Countercultural Mister Rogers* (Louisville, KY: Westminster John Knox Press, 2015), 167, 157–58.

66 **empathy for animals**: Maxwell King, *The Good Neighbor: The Life and Work of Fred Rogers* (New York: Abrams, 2018), 9.

66 **Thomas Aquinas's view**: Charlie Camosy, *For Love of Animals* (Cincinnati: Franciscan Media, 2013), 66.

67 **puppets tap into**: Victoria Nelson, *The Secret Life of Puppets* (Cambridge: Harvard University Press, 2001), 30.

67 **therapeutic puppets**: Mark I. West, "Fred Rogers and the Early Use of Puppetry on American Children's Television" in *Revising* Mister Rogers' Neighborhood: *Essays on Lessons About Self and Community* (Jefferson, NC: McFarland and Company, 2016), 151.

68 **"ecological literacy"**: Sidney I. Dobrin, "'It's Not Easy Being Green': Jim Henson, the Muppets, and Ecological Literacy" in *Wild Things: Children's Culture and Ecocriticism*, eds. Sidney I. Dobrin and Kenneth B. Kidd (Detroit: Wayne State University Press, 2004), 233, 242.

68 **a goat, William**: *Mister Rogers' Neighborhood*, #1620, "Caring for the Environment: Making Toys from Throw-Aways," performed by Fred Rogers, aired April 20, 1990, PBS.

72 **"Talks about Families"**: *Mister Rogers' Neighborhood*, #1551–1555, series "Mister Rogers Talks About Families," performed by Fred Rogers, aired November 25–29, 1985, PBS.

74 **shows children his puppets**: *Mister Rogers' Neighborhood*, #1384, performed by Fred Rogers, aired May 9, 1974, PBS.

75 **"the doubleness of the puppet"**: Kenneth Gross, "The Madness of Puppets," *Hopkins Review* 2, no. 2 (2009): 192, doi:10.1353/thr.0.0066.

77 **"the king's self-involved authoritarianism"**: Susan Linn, "With an Open Hand: Puppetry on Mister Rogers' Neighborhood," in *Mister Rogers Neighborhood: Children Television and Fred Rogers*, eds. Mark Collins and Margaret Mary Kimmel (Pittsburgh: University of Pittsburgh Press, 1996), 98, doi:10.2307/j.ctt5hjsmz.11, 91.

77 **neither are silent**: Zoe Jaques, *Children's Literature and the Posthuman: Animal, Environment, Cyborg* (New York: Routledge, 2015), 85.

78	**cyborg**: Donna Haraway, "A Cyborg Manifesto: Science, Technology, and Socialist-Feminism in the Late Twentieth Century," in *Simians, Cyborgs and Women: The Reinvention of Nature* (New York: Routledge, 1991), 155.
79	**listening to silent animals**: Jaques, *Children's Literature and the Posthuman*, 104.
79	**"humankind"**: Timothy Morton, *Humankind: In Solidarity with Nonhuman People* (New York: Verso, 2017), 137, 138, 143, 189.
80	**swim every morning**: King, *The Good Neighbor*, 317.
80	**daily "baptism"**: Amy Hollingsworth, *The Simple Faith of Mister Rogers: Spiritual Insights from the World's Most Beloved Neighbor* (Nashville: Thomas Nelson, 2005), 20.
80	**"the model of conversion"**: Shea Tuttle, *Exactly as You Are: The Life and Faith of Mister Rogers* (Grand Rapids, MI: William B. Eerdmans Publishing Company, 2019), 107, 129.

Chapter Four: Playthings and Creativity: Reduce, Reuse, Recycle, and Co-Create

83	**"open-ended"**: Fred Rogers, The Mister Rogers Parenting Resource Book: Helping to Understand Your Young Child and Encourage Learning and Pretending (Philadelphia: Courage Books, 2005), 26.
83	**play helps children**: David Elkind, The Power of Play: Learning What Comes Naturally (Boston: Da Capo Lifelong Books), 2007.
83	**"Sustained attention to things"**: Fred Rogers, You Are Special: Words of Wisdom from America's Most Beloved Neighbor (New York: Viking, 1994), 91.
83	**"single action" toys**: Rogers, Parenting Resource Book, 26.
84	**"interactive fascination"**: Jane Bennett, The Enchantment of Modern Life: Attachments, Crossings, and Ethics (Princeton: Princeton University Press, 2001), 3, 4, 5, 10.
84	**"flexible form of pedagogy"**: Sarah Anne Carter, "An Object Lesson, or Don't Eat the Evidence," Journal of the History of Childhood and Youth 3, no. 1 (2010), 7, 8, 9.
84	**"recycling advice"**: Mister Rogers' Neighborhood, #1616, "Caring for the Environment: Reduce, Reuse, Recycle," performed by Fred Rogers, aired April 16, 1990, PBS.
86	**"entangles us in responsibility"**: Stacy Alaimo, Exposed: Environmental Politics and Pleasures in Posthuman Times (Minneapolis: University of Minnesota Press, 2016), 4.
89	**Daniel Tiger**: Mister Rogers' Neighborhood, #1578, "Making Mistakes," performed by Fred Rogers, aired May 6, 1987, PBS.

90 **"life-enhancing gift"**: Fred Rogers, "PBS Development Conference," Tucson, Arizona (Latrobe, PA: Fred Rogers Archives, 1991).

90 **"one-of-a-kind"**: Fred Rogers, "TV Critics Speech" (Latrobe, PA: Fred Rogers Archives, 1998).

91 **"radical interdependence"**: Tim Libretti, "Dis-Alienating the Neighborhood: The Representation of Work and Community," in *Revisiting Mister Rogers' Neighborhood: Essays on Lessons About Self and Community*, eds. Kathy Merlock Jackson and Steven M. Emmanuel (Jefferson, NC: McFarland and Company, 2016), 61, 63.

94 **wood puzzle box**: *Mister Rogers' Neighborhood*, #1618, "Caring for the Environment: Caring for our Planet by Recycling," performed by Fred Rogers, aired April 18, 1990, PBS.

96 **ecological philosophy**: Timothy Morton, *Being Ecological* (London: Penguin, 2018), 50–51, 52.

97 **"paradoxes about omnipotence"**: Rogers, *Special*, 170.

100 **"sane design for living"**: Rogers, "Encouraging Creativity."

100 **"creative endeavors"**: Fred Rogers, "Nurturing Creative Energy," *New York Times*, August 21, 1983.

100 **radical theology**: Guy, "Theology," 108.

101 **"partners with God"**: Rogers, "Memphis."

Chapter Five: "Tree Tree Tree": The Joy in Rogers's Ecological Worldview

107 **younger sister**: *Mister Rogers' Neighborhood*, #1135, performed by Fred Rogers, aired February 19, 1971, PBS.

108 **Lady Elaine turns things upside down**: *Mister Rogers' Neighborhood*, #0030, performed by Fred Rogers, aired March 29, 1968, PBS.

109 **opera about a mother**: *Mister Rogers' Neighborhood*, #0045, performed by Fred Rogers, aired April 19, 1968, PBS.

109 **Yo-Yo Ma's famous visit**: *Mister Rogers' Neighborhood*, #1547, "Mister Rogers Talks About Music," performed by Fred Rogers, aired May 14, 1985, PBS.

110 **Finnish singer, Barbara Koski**: *Mister Rogers' Neighborhood*, #1056, performed by Fred Rogers, aired April 28, 1969, PBS.

110 **Ukrainian American Peter Ostroushko**: *Mister Rogers' Neighborhood*, #1664, "Mister Rogers Talks About Love," performed by Fred Rogers, aired February 25, 1993, PBS.

110 **Dean Shostak**: *Mister Rogers' Neighborhood*, #1764, "Mister Rogers Celebrates the Arts," performed by Fred Rogers, aired August 30, 2001, PBS.

Notes

112 **"The Neighborhood Archive"**: Tim Lybarger, *The Neighborhood Archive: All Things Mister Rogers*, accessed October 23, 2019, http://www.neighborhoodarchive.com.

114 **daily swim**: Hollingsworth, *Simple Faith*, 20.

114 **the doxology or silence**: Ibid., 13.

115 **lowest life form**: Randy Laist, ed., "Introduction," *Plants and Literature: Essays in Critical Plant Studies* (New York: Rodopi, 2013), 13.

115 **"plant blindness"**: Christine Ro, "Why 'Plant Blindness' Matters—and What You Can Do About It," *BBC Future*, April 29, 2019, http://www.bbc.com/future/story/20190425-plant-blindness-what-we-lose-with-nature-deficit-disorder.

116 **from 1969**: *Mister Rogers' Neighborhood*, #1030, performed by Fred Rogers, aired March 21, 1969, PBS.

116 **"back at the house"**: Tim Lybarger, "Episode 1030," *The Neighborhood Archive: All Things Mister Rogers*, http://www.neighborhoodarchive.com/mrn/episodes/1030/index.html.

117 **Don Riggs**: *Mister Rogers' Neighborhood*, #1152, performed by Fred Rogers, aired March 17, 1971, PBS, retrieved via Vimeo, https://vimeo.com/288241402.

117 **Negri's Music Shop**: Tim Lybarger, "Episode 1152," *The Neighborhood Archive: All Things Mister Rogers*, http://www.neighborhoodarchive.com/mrn/episodes/1152/index.html.

117 **this 1971 episode**: *Mister Rogers' Neighborhood*, #1152, performed by Fred Rogers, aired March 17, 1971, PBS, retrieved via Vimeo, https://vimeo.com/288241402.

118 **"Friends" in 1982**: *Mister Rogers' Neighborhood*, #1509, "Mister Rogers Talks About Friends," performed by Fred Rogers, aired November 18, 1982, PBS.

119 **In the 1974 instance**: *Mister Rogers' Neighborhood*, #1364, performed by Fred Rogers, aired April 11, 1974, PBS.

119 **"brown sugar syrup"**: Tim Lybarger, "Episode 1364," *The Neighborhood Archive: All Things Mister Rogers*, http://www.neighborhoodarchive.com/mrn/episodes/1364/index.html.

121 **twice on Monday**: *Mister Rogers' Neighborhood*, #1761, "Mister Rogers Celebrates the Arts," performed by Fred Rogers, aired August 27, 2001, PBS.

121 **once on Thursday**: *Mister Rogers' Neighborhood*, #1764, "Mister Rogers Celebrates the Arts," performed by Fred Rogers, aired August 30, 2001, PBS.

123 **In 2000**: *Mister Rogers' Neighborhood*, #1755, "Mister Rogers Talks About Curiosity," performed by Fred Rogers, aired February 12, 2000, PBS.

Conclusion: Fred Rogers and Environmental Wisdom

125 **Winnie Palmer Nature Preserve**: Angela Belli, interviewed by authors, Latrobe, PA, May 29, 2019.

125 **environmental play**: See the Winnie Palmer Nature Preserve at Saint Vincent College, https://www.wpnr.org.

125 **self-directed play**: Carin Vadala, Robert Bixler, and J. Joy James, "Childhood Play and Environmental Interests: Panacea or Snake Oil?," *Journal of Environmental Education* 39, no. 1 (2007): 3–17.

127 **"solve the problem"**: Fred Rogers, Hedda Sharapan, and Roberta Schomburg, "Activities for Young Children About the Environment and Recycling" (Pittsburgh: Family Communications, 1990), 7.

128 **"protection and support"**: Fred Rogers, "The Mister Rogers' Neighborhood Assassination Special" (Pittsburgh: WQED, June 7, 1968), https://archive.org/details/youtube-juwdeDzjVCQ.

129 **"the foundation of our very being"**: Fred Rogers, "Commencement Address for Saint Vincent College" (Latrobe, PA: Fred Rogers Archives, 2000), 7.

129 **"sure thing about anyone's future"**: Rogers, "Barley," 7.

129 **"young, wise Freddy"**: Tuttle, *Exactly as You Are*, 11.

130 **"behind the things"**: Fred Rogers, "More Than We Know," principal address at the Opening Ceremonies of the Sesquicentennial of Saint Vincent, Saint Vincent Archabbey Basilica (Latrobe, PA: Fred Rogers Archives, April 25, 1995), 3–4.

130 **what wisdom can do**: Fred Rogers, "Invisible Essentials" (Latrobe, PA: Fred Rogers Archives, 1997), 2.

Bibliography

Alaimo, Stacy. *Exposed: Environmental Politics and Pleasures in Posthuman Times*. Minneapolis: University of Minnesota Press, 2016.
Belli, Angela. Interviewed by authors, Latrobe, PA. May 29, 2019.
Bennett, Jane. *The Enchantment of Modern Life: Attachments, Crossings, and Ethics*. Princeton: Princeton University Press, 2001.
Bennett, Jane. "Systems and Things: On Vital Materialism and Object-Oriented Philosophy." In *The Nonhuman Turn*, edited by Richard Grusin, 223–39. Minneapolis: University of Minnesota Press, 2015.
Boersema, David. "The Virtues of Art." In *Mister Rogers and Philosophy: Wondering Through the Neighborhood*, edited by Eric J. Mohr and Holly K. Mohr, 67–74. Chicago: Open Court, 2020.
Buczinsky, Chris. "The Performance of the Pastoral." In *Revisiting Mister Rogers' Neighborhood: Essays on Lessons About Self and Community*, edited by Kathy Merlock Jackson and Steven M. Emmanuel, 3–11. Jefferson, NC: McFarland and Company, 2015.
Camosy, Charlie. *For Love of Animals*. Cincinnati: Franciscan Media, 2013.
Carter, Sarah Anne. "An Object Lesson, or Don't Eat the Evidence." *Journal of the History of Childhood and Youth* 3, no. 1 (2010): 7–12.
Curry, Nancy E. "The Reality of Make-Believe." In *Mister Rogers Neighborhood: Children Television and Fred Rogers*, edited by Mark Collins and Margaret Mary Kimmel, 51–64. Pittsburgh: University of Pittsburgh Press, 1996.
Deitering, Cynthia. "The Postnatural Novel: Toxic Consciousness in Fiction of the 1980s." In *The Ecocriticism Reader: Landmarks in Literary Ecology*, edited by Cheryll Glotfelty and Harold Fromm, 196–203. Athens: University of Georgia Press, 1996.
Dobrin, Sidney I. "'It's Not Easy Being Green': Jim Henson, the Muppets, and Ecological Literacy." In *Wild Things: Children's Culture and Ecocriticism*, edited by Sidney I. Dobrin and Kenneth B. Kidd, 232–53. Detroit: Wayne State University Press, 2004.

Dobrin, Sidney I., and Kenneth B. Kidd. "Introduction: Into the Wild." In *Wild Things: Children's Culture and Ecocriticism*, edited by Sidney I. Dobrin and Kenneth B. Kidd, 183–97. Detroit: Wayne State University Press, 2004.

Echterling, Clare. "How to Save the World and Other Lessons from Children's Environmental Literature." *Children's Literature in Education* 47, no. 4 (2016): 283–99.

Edwards, Gavin. *Kindness and Wonder: Why Mister Rogers Matters Now More Than Ever*. New York: HarperCollins, 2019.

Elkind, David. *The Power of Play: Learning What Comes Naturally*. Boston: Da Capo Lifelong Books, 2007.

Francis. *Laudato Si'*. Washington, DC: United States Conference of Catholic Bishops, 2015.

Galinsky, Ellen. "Mister Rogers Speaks to Parents." In *Mister Rogers Neighborhood: Children Television and Fred Rogers*, edited by Mark Collins and Margaret Mary Kimmel, 163–74. Pittsburgh: University of Pittsburgh Press, 1996.

Gilmore, Timothy. "After the Apocalypse: Wildness as Preservative in a Time of Ecological Crisis." *ISLE: Interdisciplinary Studies in Literature and Environment*, 24, no. 3 (2017): 389–413.

Gross, Kenneth. "The Madness of Puppets." *Hopkins Review* 2, no. 2 (2009): 182–205.

Guy, William. "The Theology of *Mister Rogers' Neighborhood*." In *Mister Rogers Neighborhood: Children Television and Fred Rogers*, edited by Mark Collins and Margaret Mary Kimmel, 101–121. Pittsburgh: University of Pittsburgh Press, 1996.

Haraway, Donna. "A Cyborg Manifesto: Science, Technology, and Socialist-Feminism in the Late Twentieth Century." In *Simians, Cyborgs and Women: The Reinvention of Nature*, 149–81. New York: Routledge, 1991.

Hollingsworth, Amy. *The Simple Faith of Mister Rogers: Spiritual Insights from the World's Most Beloved Neighbor*. Nashville: Thomas Nelson, 2005.

Jackson, Kathy Merlock. "Social Activism for the Small Set," In *Revisiting Mister Rogers' Neighborhood: Essays on Lessons About Self and Community*, edited by Kathy Merlock Jackson and Steven M. Emmanuel, 12–23. Jefferson, NC: McFarland and Company, 2015.

James, J. Joy, and Robert D. Bixler. "Children's Role in Meaning Making Through Their Participation in an Environmental Education Program." *Journal of Environmental Education* 39, no. 4 (2008): 44–59.

Jaques, Zoe. *Children's Literature and the Posthuman: Animal, Environment, Cyborg*. New York: Routledge, 2015.

Kiel, Micah. *Apocalyptic Ecology: The Book of Revelation, the Earth, and the Future*. Minnesota: Liturgical Press, 2017.

King, Maxwell. *The Good Neighbor: The Life and Work of Fred Rogers.* New York: Abrams, 2018.

Laist, Randy, ed. "Introduction." *Plants and Literature: Essays in Critical Plant Studies,* 9–17. New York: Rodopi, 2013.

Larkin, Susan. "Fantasy as Free-Space: Mister Rogers' Neighborhoods." In *Revisiting* Mister Rogers' Neighborhood: *Essays on Lessons About Self and Community,* edited by Kathy Merlock Jackson and Steven M. Emmanuel, 76–87. Jefferson, NC: McFarland and Company, 2016.

Libretti, Tim. "Dis-Alienating the Neighborhood: The Representation of Work and Community." In *Revisiting Mister Rogers' Neighborhood: Essays on Lessons About Self and Community,* edited by Kathy Merlock Jackson and Steven M. Emmanuel, 59–75. Jefferson, NC: McFarland and Company, 2016.

Linn, Susan. "With an Open Hand: Puppetry on *Mister Rogers' Neighborhood.*" In *Mister Rogers Neighborhood: Children Television and Fred Rogers,* edited by Mark Collins and Margaret Mary Kimmel, 89–99. Pittsburgh: University of Pittsburgh Press, 1996.

Long, Michael. *Peaceful Neighbor: Discovering the Countercultural Mister Rogers.* Westminster: John Knox Press, 2015.

Lybarger, Tim. "Episode 1030." *The Neighborhood Archive: All Things Mister Rogers.* Accessed October 23, 2019. http://www.neighborhoodarchive.com/mrn/episodes/1030/index.html.

Lybarger, Tim. "Episode 1152." *The Neighborhood Archive: All Things Mister Rogers.* Accessed October 23, 2019. http://www.neighborhoodarchive.com/mrn/episodes/1152/index.html.

Lybarger, Tim. "Episode 1364." *The Neighborhood Archive: All Things Mister Rogers.* Accessed October 23, 2019. http://www.neighborhoodarchive.com/mrn/episodes/1364/index.html.

Lybarger, Tim. *The Neighborhood Archive: All Things Mister Rogers.* Accessed October 23, 2019. http://www.neighborhoodarchive.com.

Mackey, Glynne. "To Know, To Decide, To Act: The Young Child's Right to Participate in Action for the Environment." *Environmental Education Research* 18, no. 4 (2012): 473–84.

Marder, Michael. *Plant-Thinking: A Philosophy of Vegetal Life.* New York: Columbia University Press, 2013.

Marion, Jean-Luc. *God without Being.* Translated by Thomas Carlson. Chicago: University of Chicago Press, 1991.

McMahon, Christopher. "Imaginative Faith: Apocalyptic, Science Fiction Theory, and Theology." *Dialogue: A Journal of Theology* 47, no. 3 (2008): 271–77.

Moo, Jonathan. "Climate Change and the Apocalyptic Imagination: Science, Faith, and Ecological Responsibility." *Zygon* 50, no. 4 (2015): 937–48.

Morton, Timothy. *Being Ecological.* London: Penguin, 2018.

Morton, Timothy. *Humankind: In Solidarity with Nonhuman People*. New York: Verso, 2017.

Nelson, Victoria. *The Secret Life of Puppets*. Cambridge: Harvard University Press, 2001.

Nixon, Rob. *Slow Violence and the Environmentalism of the Poor*. Cambridge: Harvard University Press, 2011.

Pelo, Ann. "A Sense of Wonder: Cultivating an Ecological Identity in Young Children—and in Ourselves." *Canadian Children* 39, no. 2 (2014): 5–18.

Platt, Kamala. "Environmental Justice Children's Literature: Depicting, Defending, and Celebrating Trees and Birds, Colors and People." In *Wild Things: Children's Culture and Ecocriticism*, edited by Sidney I. Dobrin and Kenneth B. Kidd, 183–97. Detroit: Wayne State University Press, 2004.

Rogers, Fred. "Caring for Our Planet: Care That's Caught." Latrobe, PA: Fred Rogers Archives, 1990.

Rogers, Fred. "Commencement Address for Saint Vincent College." Latrobe, PA: Fred Rogers Archives, 2000.

Rogers, Fred. "Encouraging Creativity: Theil College Commencement Address." Latrobe, PA: Fred Rogers Archives, 1969.

Rogers, Fred. "Invisible Essentials: Memphis Theological Seminary Address." Latrobe, PA: Fred Rogers Archives, 1997.

Rogers, Fred. "Invisible to the Eye: Johnson & Johnson Speech." Latrobe, PA: Fred Rogers Archives, 1994.

Rogers, Fred. "The Mister Rogers' Neighborhood Assassination Special." Pittsburgh: WQED, June 7, 1968. https://archive.org/details/youtube-juwdeDzjVCQ.

Rogers, Fred, creator. *Mister Rogers' Neighborhood*. #0030. Aired March 29, 1968, PBS.

Rogers, Fred, creator. *Mister Rogers' Neighborhood*. #0045. Aired April 19, 1968, PBS.

Rogers, Fred, creator. *Mister Rogers' Neighborhood*. #1030. Aired March 21, 1969, PBS.

Rogers, Fred, creator. *Mister Rogers' Neighborhood*. #1056. Aired April 28, 1969, PBS.

Rogers, Fred, creator. *Mister Rogers' Neighborhood*. #1135. Aired February 19, 1971, PBS.

Rogers, Fred, creator. *Mister Rogers' Neighborhood*. #1152. Aired March 17, 1971, PBS.

Rogers, Fred, creator. *Mister Rogers' Neighborhood*. #1205. Aired March 3, 1972, PBS.

Rogers, Fred, creator. *Mister Rogers' Neighborhood*. #1364. Aired April 11, 1974, PBS.

Rogers, Fred, creator. *Mister Rogers' Neighborhood*. #1509, "Mister Rogers Talks About Friends." Aired November 18, 1982, PBS.
Rogers, Fred, creator. *Mister Rogers' Neighborhood*. #1547, "Mister Rogers Talks About Music." Aired May 14, 1985, PBS.
Rogers, Fred, creator. *Mister Rogers' Neighborhood*. #1551–1555, series "Mister Rogers Talks About Families." Aired November 25–29, 1985, PBS.
Rogers, Fred, creator. *Mister Rogers' Neighborhood*. #1616, "Caring for the Environment: Reduce, Reuse, Recycle." Aired April 16, 1990, PBS.
Rogers, Fred, creator. *Mister Rogers' Neighborhood*. #1617, "Caring for the Environment: A Visit to a Recycling Center." Aired April 17, 1990, PBS.
Rogers, Fred, creator. *Mister Rogers' Neighborhood*. #1618, "Caring for the Environment: Caring for our Planet by Recycling." Aired April 18, 1990, PBS.
Rogers, Fred, creator. *Mister Rogers' Neighborhood*. #1619, "Caring for the Environment: Snorkeling with Sylvia Earle." Aired April 19, 1990, PBS.
Rogers, Fred, creator. *Mister Rogers' Neighborhood*. #1620, "Caring for the Environment: Making Toys from Throw-Aways." Aired April 20, 1990, PBS.
Rogers, Fred, creator. *Mister Rogers' Neighborhood*. #1664, "Mister Rogers Talks About Love." Aired February 25, 1993, PBS.
Rogers, Fred, creator. *Mister Rogers' Neighborhood*. #1755, "Mister Rogers Talks About Curiosity." Aired February 12, 2000, PBS.
Rogers, Fred, creator. *Mister Rogers' Neighborhood*. #1761, "Mister Rogers Celebrates the Arts." Aired August 27, 2001, PBS.
Rogers, Fred, creator. *Mister Rogers' Neighborhood*. #1764, "Mister Rogers Celebrates the Arts." Aired August 30, 2001, PBS.
Rogers, Fred. "More Than We Know," principal address at the opening ceremonies of the sesquicentennial of Saint Vincent, Saint Vincent Archabbey Basilica. Latrobe, PA: Fred Rogers Archives, April 25, 1995.
Rogers, Fred. "Nurturing Creative Energy." *New York Times*, August 21, 1983. Latrobe, PA: Fred Rogers Archives, 1983.
Rogers, Fred. "PBS Development Conference," Tucson Arizona. Latrobe, PA: Fred Rogers Archives, 1991.
Rogers, Fred. "Sermon for Installation of the Reverend Kenneth Barley." Latrobe, PA: Fred Rogers Archives, 1989.
Rogers, Fred. "TV Critics Speech." Latrobe, PA: Fred Rogers Archives, 1998.
Rogers, Fred. *You Are Special: Words of Wisdom from America's Most Beloved Neighbor*. New York: Viking, 1994.
Ro, Christine. "Why 'Plant Blindness' Matters—and What You Can Do About It." *BBC Future*, April 29, 2019. http://www.bbc.com/future/story/20190425-plant-blindness-what-we-lose-with-nature-deficit-disorder.
Saint-Exupéry, Antoine de. *The Little Prince*. Translated by Richard Howard. Boston: Mariner Books, 2000.

Scott, Rebecca. *Removing Mountains: Extracting Nature and Identity in the Appalachia Coalfields*. Minneapolis: University of Minnesota Press, 2010.

Starosielski, Nicole. "Beyond Fluidity: A Cultural History of Cinema Under Water." In *Ecocinema Theory and Practice*, edited by Stephen Rust, Salma Monani, and Sean Cubitt, 149–68. New York: Routledge, 2013.

Strife, Susan Jean. "Children's Environmental Concerns: Expressing Ecophobia." *Journal of Environmental Education* 43, no. 1 (2012): 37–54.

Tucker, Mary Evelyn. "Globalization, Catholic Social Teaching, and the Environment." *Journal of Catholic Social Thought* 4, no. 2 (2007): 355–71.

Tuttle, Shea. *Exactly as You Are: The Life and Faith of Mister Rogers*. Grand Rapids, MI: William B. Eerdmans Publishing Company, 2019.

Ussia, Matthew. "Mister Rogers's Lessons for Democracy." In *Mister Rogers and Philosophy: Wondering Through the Neighborhood*, edited by Eric J. Mohr and Holly K. Mohr, 185–94. Chicago: Open Court, 2020.

Veldman, Robin. "Narrating the Environmental Apocalypse." *Ethics & the Environment* 17, no. 1 (2012): 1–23.

West, Mark I. "Fred Rogers and the Early Use of Puppetry on American Children's Television." In *Revising* Mister Rogers' Neighborhood: *Essays on Lessons About Self and Community*, edited by Kathy Merlock Jackson and Steven M. Emmanuel, 146–52. Jefferson, NC: McFarland and Company, 2016.

Whitelaw, Jessica. "Beyond the Bedtime Story: In Search of Epistemic Possibilities and the Innovative Potential of Disquieting Picturebooks." *Bookbird: A Journal of International Children's Literature* 55, no. 1 (2017): 33–41.

Whitman, Walt. *Leaves of Grass: The First (1855) Edition*. New York: Penguin Books, 2005.

Index

Aber, Chuck "Neighbor," 21, 68, 78, 140, 142–43
Aberlin, Betty (Lady), 27–29, 31, 33–34, 48, 68–69, 71, 74, 80, 92–93, 108, 136, 138, 140–42
activism, 39–40, 45, 130, 153, 160; environmental, 39, 55, 60, 79, 101; environmental action, 37–38, 40, 54–56, 92, 96, 99, 103, 123, 126, 129–31
"Activities for Young Children about the Environment and Recycling," 14–15, 126, 150, 158
Alaimo, Stacy, 86, 155, 159
Ana Platypus, 72–73, 127
anger, 9, 128–29
animals, 7, 16–18, 22, 31–32, 35, 38, 42, 48, 51, 54–55, 61, 63–74, 76, 78–81, 89, 91, 99, 117, 122–23, 126, 138, 141, 154–55, 159–60; wisdom of, 32, 63, 68–71, 81; birds, 37–39, 51, 73, 122, 137, 150, 153, 162, 164; fish, 16–17, 33, 43–44, 46–57, 65–66, 78–80, 91, 122–24, 126, 130, 133, 135, 138–42; goats, 15–17, 21, 28–29, 31, 33–35, 40, 57, 63, 65, 68–71, 80, 130, 138, 140–43, 154
anxiety, 22, 27–28, 30, 77, 112, 128–29
apocalypticism, 17, 22–23, 31–32, 35, 37, 40, 42, 80, 128, 150–52, 160–61, 164;
biblical, 23, 32, 37, 152; and ecology, 32, 151–52, 160; and environtalism, 21–23, 31, 150
art and artists, ix, 46, 14–15, 16–18, 43–48, 50–61, 76, 94, 101, 121–22, 126, 130, 138, 145, 153, 157, 159

Barnett, Marilyn, 85, 134
Belli, Angela, 125, 158–59
Bennett, Jane, 61, 84, 153, 155, 159
Betty Okonak Templeton, 33, 72, 74, 138
Bixler, Robert, 39, 125, 152, 158, 160
Bob Dog, 24, 31, 33, 72–73, 134
Boersema, David, 45, 153, 159
Buczinsky, Chris, 14, 53, 150, 153, 159

care, 4, 8–9, 12, 15–18, 28, 30–32, 35, 37, 38, 40, 44–45, 48, 50–52, 54–56, 60–61, 63, 65–67, 71, 73, 76, 78–81, 86–87, 90–92, 94, 97, 99, 101, 103, 106, 109, 116–20, 124–26, 128–31, 135, 137, 139–41, 152, 162
"Caring for Our Planet: Care That's Caught," 36, 137, 152–53, 156, 162–63
"Caring for the Environment," xii, 14–18, 21, 23, 36, 40, 43–44, 53–54, 60, 63, 65, 68, 75, 79, 80, 84, 92, 95,

98–99, 101, 106, 116, 118–19, 126–28, 130, 133, 151–56, 163
Carter, Sarah Anne, 84, 155, 159
"Celebrating the Arts," 121
Chef Brockett, 119
climate change, 22, 161
collaboration, 4, 28, 59, 95, 101, 111, 145
community, 12, 26, 32–33, 35, 39, 40, 45, 68, 70, 85, 90, 101, 111, 114, 128, 130, 150, 152–54, 156, 159–61, 164
compassion, 4, 56, 67, 79, 146
conflict, 29, 42, 77
contemplation, 5, 45, 59
conversation, 29–30, 61, 68–69, 84
conversion, 57, 63–67, 69, 80, 154–55
cooperation, 11, 26, 37, 63, 78
Cornflake S. Pecially (Corny), 40–41, 67, 76, 91–93, 136
Costa, Johnny, 48, 117–18
creativity, 5, 14, 31, 37, 40, 45, 47, 57, 83, 98, 100–101, 111, 129, 150, 153, 155–56, 162–63
curiosity, 5, 48, 56, 123, 139, 147, 157, 163
cyborg, 76, 78, 154–55, 160

Daniel Striped Tiger, 67, 76, 89, 127–28, 155
Deitering, Cynthia, 25–26, 151, 159
development, xi, xii, 5–6, 8, 42, 83, 156, 163
dignity, 4, 48, 50–51, 66, 68–69, 71, 73
Dobrin, Sidney, 16, 67, 150, 154, 159–60, 162
Donkey Hodie, 17, 24–26, 127, 134, 142
doxology, 114, 146, 157

Earle, Sylvia, 16, 47–49, 52–56, 139, 151, 153, 163
earth, 7, 9, 14, 16, 21–22, 41, 53–54, 65, 99–101, 111, 120, 151, 160
Echterling, Clare, 22, 151, 160

ecology: apocalyptic, 32, 151–53, 159–60; and consciousness, 3, 15, 17–18, 31, 49, 63, 65, 96, 107, 117, 130; conversion about, 63, 65, 67, 69, 78, 80, 154; integral, 43, 53–54, 60, 152–53; and play, 84–85, 90, 92–93, 106, 118–20
ecophobia, 128, 151, 164
ecosystems, 4, 49, 54–55, 67, 70, 96, 116, 128, 153
Edwards, Gavin, 3, 149, 160
Elkind, David, 83, 155, 160
emotions, 4–8, 17, 42, 48, 78, 81, 83, 112, 116–17
empathy, 4, 33, 35, 50, 52, 66, 67, 69, 79, 116, 126, 154
"Encouraging Creativity," 9, 45, 99, 150, 153, 156, 162
environment, xiv, 22, 30–31, 36, 38–40, 42, 44, 53, 56, 60, 65, 80, 92, 95, 106, 124–26, 128, 151–56, 158–64
environmentalism, 4, 21–23, 43, 45, 49, 68, 106, 150–52, 162; apocalyptic, 21–23, 31, 150; awareness of, 9, 11, 16, 25–26, 28, 31, 35, 55, 65, 68, 90, 100; and justice, 16, 150, 162; wisdom, 125, 129, 131, 158
"Everybody's Fancy," 51–52, 113, 117, 141

faith, 13, 14, 27, 64, 66, 80, 114, 155, 160–61, 164, 168
family, xi, 8, 17–18, 36, 49, 53, 55–56, 67, 71, 73, 76–77, 81, 87, 91, 96, 107, 109, 111, 122, 126, 146–47, 149–50, 158, 168
fantasy, 21, 29, 42, 73, 152, 161
fear, 22–23, 30, 108, 111, 128–29
feeling(s), 6, 8–9, 12–13, 18, 27, 30, 43, 45, 48–49, 51, 56, 60, 66–67, 76–77, 84, 89, 92, 95, 97, 99, 101–3, 110–13, 126–28, 130, 150
"Fish, fish, fish," 122–23
forgiveness, 10, 65, 101
Fred Rogers Center, xi, xii, xiv, 145

Index

Gilmore, Timothy, 31, 151, 160
Gross, Kenneth, 75, 154, 160
Guy, William, 11, 13, 100, 150, 156, 160

habitat, 16–17, 22, 46, 48, 53, 55
Haraway, Donna, 78, 155, 160
Harriet Elizabeth Cow, 17, 24–25, 127, 134
Henrietta Pussycat, 76, 122, 127
Hilda Dingleboarder, 17, 21, 31, 34–35, 57–58, 91, 136, 138, 142–43
Hollingsworth, Amy, 80, 114, 155, 157, 160
hope, 3, 15, 22–23, 30, 32–37, 39–40, 42, 52, 57, 77, 81, 101–3, 112, 127, 129–31, 138, 141

"I Like to Take Care of You," 91–92, 106, 135, 137
imagination, 3, 4, 8, 17–18, 31, 34, 38, 40, 44–45, 47, 49, 54, 63, 69, 83–84, 92, 94, 101–2, 107, 115–17, 129–30, 149, 161
"I'm Proud of You," 60, 113, 143
"I'm Taking Care of You," 112
instruments, 67, 110–11, 117–18, 121, 123
interdependence, 11, 14, 30, 52, 54–55, 70, 90, 98, 151, 156; entanglement, 32, 86, 130, 155; interconnected, 18, 53, 57, 73, 93, 130
invisible essentials, 4–14, 31, 52–53, 61, 84, 130–31, 149–50, 158, 162
"Invisible Essentials," 4, 6, 10–14, 150, 158, 162
"Invisible to the Eye," 5, 7, 8, 10, 12–13, 149, 162
"It's Afternoon, Let's Sing About It!," 108
"It's Such a Good Feeling" (closing song), 96, 101–2, 112, 117, 121, 133, 137, 139, 141, 143
"It's You I Like," 10, 113

James, J. Joy, 39, 125, 152, 158, 160
Jaques, Zoe, 79, 154–55, 160
joy, 4–6, 10, 18, 39, 47, 54, 65, 67, 84, 86, 101, 103, 105, 107–9, 111–14, 115, 117, 119–21, 123, 125, 152
"Jubilate Deo," 114

Kidd, Kenneth, 16, 150, 154, 159, 160, 162
Kiel, Micah, 23, 151, 160
kindness, 5, 64, 146, 149, 160
King, Maxwell, 5, 66, 145, 149, 154, 161
King Friday XIII, 21, 23–25, 27, 29–31, 33–34, 41, 57, 58–60, 65, 71, 75–77, 80, 96, 98–99, 108, 119, 134, 136, 138, 140–43
Koski, Barbara, 18, 110, 156

Lady Elaine Fairchilde, 21, 28, 33, 48, 56, 80, 98
Larkin, Susan, 42, 152, 161
Latrobe, PA, xi, 125, 149–54, 156, 158–59, 162–63, 167–68
Laudato Si: On Care for Our Common Home, 54, 65, 153–54, 160
Li, Junlei, xi–xv, 29
Linn, Susan, 77, 154, 161
Little Prince, The (Saint-Exupéry) 7–8, 12, 149, 163
Long, Michael, 6, 66, 149, 154, 161
love, 6–7, 9–13, 15, 22–23, 30, 32, 36–37, 44, 55, 64–67, 70, 73, 76–79, 84–85, 89, 91–92, 97, 99, 101, 105–19, 122–24, 129–30, 139, 147, 150, 154–56, 159–60, 163, 168; "love-ethic," 11, 13, 150, 159
Lybarger, Tim, 112, 116, 119–20, 157, 161

Ma, Yo-Yo, 13, 18, 109, 156
Mackey, Glynne, 38, 152, 161
"Many Ways to Say I Love You," 113, 118
Mary Owl, 72, 122
Mayor Maggie, 30, 98, 122, 136, 138, 143

McFarland, Margaret, 5, 150, 152–54, 159–61, 164
Mister Rogers' Neighborhood, xiii, xiv, 4–5, 8–14, 16, 21, 26, 32, 61, 64–65, 72–73, 77, 84, 90, 97, 105, 107, 110–13, 116, 123, 129–30, 147, 150–57, 159–64
"Mister Rogers Talks about Families," 72, 154, 163
Morton, Timothy, 79, 96, 155–56, 161–62
Mr. McFeely, 24, 34, 38, 46–47, 57, 68–69, 84–89, 96, 121, 133–35, 137–38, 141
Mrs. McFeely, 38–40, 96, 137, 141
Mrs. Shiono, 73
music, 4–5, 13, 23–24, 48, 50, 57, 60–61, 110–12, 117–18, 123, 134, 139, 156–57, 163; song, 15, 18, 28, 45, 51, 59–61, 89, 91–92, 96, 101–2, 105–24, 133, 135, 140–41

nature, xi, 15–16, 31, 45, 50, 65–66, 80, 107–8, 112, 114–15, 118, 120–21, 124–26, 150, 151, 155, 157–58, 160, 163–64
Negri, Joe "Handyman," 18, 21–24, 30, 33, 57, 109–11, 118–19, 123, 133–34, 138, 157
Neighborhood, the, xii, xiv, xv, 3–4, 10, 15–17, 21, 23, 29, 37, 40, 42–43, 46, 48–49, 52, 55–56, 58–61, 66, 68, 74, 78–81, 90–93, 98–99, 108, 111, 113, 116, 127, 130, 133, 140–41, 150–57, 159–64
Neighborhood of Make-Believe, xiv, 15–17, 21–24, 26, 28–35, 37, 40–42, 48, 54–60, 63, 68, 70, 74, 76–80, 91, 92, 98, 108, 119, 121–22, 127–28, 133, 136, 138, 140–42, 150, 159
Nelson, Victoria, 67, 154, 162
New Goat, 34–35, 40, 69–71, 140, 142
Northwood, 15, 28–29, 31, 33–35, 57, 68, 70, 138, 140, 142

"Nurturing Creative Energy," 100, 156, 163

ocean, 16, 21, 31, 33, 46–50, 52–56, 65, 70–71, 79–80, 129–40, 142, 153
Old Goat, 31, 34–35, 40, 69–71, 138, 140, 142
Ostroushko, Peter, 18, 110–11, 156
"Owl Correspondence School," 122

Patrice (host of *The Universe Today*), 35, 57–58, 78, 140, 142–43
Pelo, Ann, 36, 152, 162
Pittsburgh, PA, xii, 5, 26, 64, 80, 107, 147, 150, 154, 158–62
plant blindness, 115–16, 157, 163
Platt, Kamala, 16, 150, 162
play, 15, 18, 21, 23, 38, 40, 42, 47–48, 56, 58–61, 66, 70, 74–77, 83–88, 90, 92–94, 96–103, 109–11, 117–20, 125, 127, 129, 134, 139, 142–43, 155, 158, 160
"Please Don't Think It's Funny," 112
pollution, 17, 26, 33, 41, 79, 86
pretend, 15, 26, 29, 32, 40, 42, 74, 99, 155
Prince Tuesday, 71, 74, 127
puppets, xiv, 4–5, 17–18, 24, 28, 35, 38, 40, 52, 56–57, 59, 63–64, 66–81, 86, 91, 96–99, 102, 126–28, 130, 141, 143, 153–54, 160–62, 164
Purple Jet, 21, 31, 98, 140
Purple Panda, 67

Queen Sara Saturday, 18, 70, 76, 110, 134, 141

recycling, 14, 15–18, 34–39, 43–44, 46–47, 53, 55, 58–59, 84–92, 94, 102, 106, 117–18, 126, 128, 135–37, 150–53, 155–56, 158, 163
relationships, xiv, 7, 11, 16, 30, 44, 46, 50, 54, 59, 65, 68, 70, 76, 79, 84–85, 90, 96–97, 99, 113–14, 124, 131

Riggs, Don, 117–18, 157
Robert Troll, 41

Saint Vincent College, xi, xiii, 11, 36, 129, 130, 145, 150, 158, 162
Schomburg, Roberta, 126, 145, 150, 158
Schussler, Elisabeth, 115–16
Scott, Rebecca, 25, 151, 164
"Sermon for Installation of the Reverend Kenneth L. Barley," 27, 129, 151, 163
Sewell, Leo (sculptor), 17, 46–47, 57, 137, 153
Sharapan, Hedda, 126, 150, 158
Shostak, Dean, 110–11, 156
Someplace Else, 16, 24–25, 56, 127, 134, 136, 140, 142
Southwood, 17, 28, 33, 74, 138, 142
"Speedy Delivery," 84, 112, 121
Starosielski, Nicole, 49, 153, 164
Strife, Susan Jean, 22, 39, 151, 152, 164
Sue Goat, 142

television, xi, xii, xiii, xiv, 3–6, 9, 12, 14, 16–18, 21, 28–31, 34–35, 37–38, 40–42, 46, 48, 52, 55, 57–58, 60–61, 64–68, 70–71, 74, 90, 92, 96–98, 107–8, 112, 119, 122–23, 128, 140–41, 143, 149–50, 154, 159–61, 164
theology, 11, 13, 100, 146, 150, 156, 160–61
toys, 18, 40, 59, 76, 83–85, 89–90, 92–93, 96, 98, 106, 119, 125–26, 130, 141, 150–55, 163
trash, 15–18, 21, 23–24, 26–31, 33–35, 42, 44, 47–48, 50, 56–57, 61, 63, 65, 68–71, 76, 80, 83, 85–88, 90–92, 99, 117, 126–28, 133–36, 138, 140–42
"Tree Tree Tree," 18, 45, 105–24, 156
trolley, 23, 28, 75, 96, 98, 102, 133–34, 136, 138, 140–41, 143
Trow, Bob, 117–18

trust, 4, 7, 13, 121, 129
Tuttle, Shea, 80, 129, 155, 158, 164
"TV Critics Speech," 90, 156, 163

Uhrin, Emily, 107
"Universal Gratitude," 58–59, 60, 99
Universe Today, The, 17, 21, 28–31, 34–35, 57–59, 70, 98–99, 140–42
Ussia, Matthew, 29–30, 151, 164

Vadala, Carin, 125, 158
vegetarianism, 66, 68, 141
Veldman, Robin, 37, 152, 164

Wandersee, James, 115
West, Mark I., 67, 154, 164
Westwood, 17, 28, 30, 33, 98, 136, 138, 142
"What Do You Do with the Mad That You Feel?," 9, 112
Whitelaw, Jessica, 50, 153, 164
Williams, Kathryn, 116
William the Goat, 34, 68–69, 141
Winnie Palmer Nature Perserve, xi, 125–26, 158
Won't You Be My Neighbor?, 29, 101
"Won't You Be My Neighbor?" (opening song), 101, 112, 121, 123, 133

X the Owl, 26–27, 33, 72–73, 76, 108, 122, 127, 136

You are Special, 97
"You are Special," 113, 139, 155, 163
"You're Growing," 113, 121
"You've Got To Do It," 113

About the Authors

Photo credit: Ana Rodriguez Castillo

Sara Lindey is professor of English at Saint Vincent College in Latrobe, Pennsylvania. She teaches widely in American literature, including environmental literature. Before her work on Fred Rogers, she published essays on nineteenth-century American print culture, particularly representations of girlhood in antislavery picture books and boys' literacy in story papers in *Children's Literature Association Quarterly*, *American Periodicals*, and the *Journal of the Midwest Modern Language Association*.

Photo credit: Alex Byers

Jason King is the Irene S. Taylor Endowed Chair for Catholic Family Studies at Saint Vincent College in Latrobe, Pennsylvania. He is the author of *Faith with Benefits* (Oxford University Press) and coedited *Sex, Love, and Families* (Liturgical) with Julie Rubio. Currently, he edits the *Journal of Moral Theology*.